WHEN WORDS FAIL

Helen Pugh
1996.

When Words Fail

God and the World of Beauty

DAVID SHEARLOCK

THE CANTERBURY PRESS
NORWICH

© David Shearlock 1996

First Published 1996 by The Canterbury Press Norwich
(a publishing imprint of Hymns Ancient & Modern Limited,
a registered charity)
St Mary's Works, St Mary's Plain,
Norwich, Norfolk, NR3 3BH

British Library Cataloguing in Publication Data

A catalogue record for this book is available
from the British Library

ISBN 1-85311-131-7

*Typeset by David Gregson Associates, Beccles, Suffolk
Printed and bound in Great Britain by
Biddles Limited, Guildford and King's Lynn*

CONTENTS

PREFACE

This is a book about God, about beauty and about ourselves. It asks, and tries to answer, the question, 'Is it possible for us to know God, or to know him better, through an understanding of aesthetics, that is, the study of what is beautiful?' It is not intended to be a textbook for professional theologians, philosophers or aesthetes, though they may find something in it which helps to throw light on some ground which lies outside their particular area of study. It is rather an exploration for those who would like to know more about how we can seek, and perhaps find, God through music, art, literature and other manifestations of beauty.

In a work of such modest size, I have had to be selective in the choice of illustrations and examples, so I have concentrated on a small number of writers, composers and painters, most of whom are British and relatively recent. Because many of my own favourites appear in these pages, there is inevitably a strongly personal flavour to the book. To have attempted to survey the whole literary, musical and artistic scene, and done justice to the creative genius of all ages, lands and cultures would clearly have been impossible within its limited compass.

Very little has been written on this subject in a way which makes it accessible to the non-specialist student or reader so I have from time to time quoted from more technical sources to give a taste of what the experts have said on these matters. If it encourages people to read more widely, then this will help to achieve one of my secondary objectives, which is to springboard readers into their own exploration of these great themes. It will become readily apparent that I owe a great debt to the innumerable writers who have stimulated my own thinking over the years, many of whose ideas I have no doubt absorbed and assimilated, and perhaps reproduced unknowingly, though I have attempted where possible to acknowledge such sources in the References which are to be found at the end of the book, immediately before the Bibliography. Quotations from Scripture are taken from the Revised Standard Version *Common Bible* unless otherwise stated.

I would like to express my indebtedness to Mrs Veronica Edwards for suggesting at the outset that this book should revolve around themes, rather than specific subjects.

My grateful thanks are also due to those who read the typescript and made a number of helpful comments:

The Right Reverend Michael Ball, Bishop of Truro.

Mr John Phillips, Consultant Architect of Truro Cathedral.

Mr David Briggs, formerly Master of the Choristers and Organist of Truro Cathedral, and Elisabeth his wife.

Mr John Miller, Lay Canon of Truro Cathedral and distinguished artist, with whom I have had several lengthy discussions.

The Reverend Canon Perran Gay, who has also added to those earlier labours by sharing with me the task of reading the proofs.

The Very Reverend Stephen Smalley, Dean of Chester.

I further acknowledge with gratitude my debt to the following:

The Warden and Staff of St Deiniol's Library, Hawarden, who provided me with their splendid facilities for study and research.

The Abbot and monks of Landévennec, who made me most welcome during a six week's stay there, when much of the drafting was done.

My colleagues of the Chapter of Truro Cathedral, who gave me every encouragement to take the sabbatical leave which included those two visits.

Finally, I would like to thank my wife, Jean, for her perceptive comments and for her patience in allowing me to disappear for weeks at a stretch or to slink off to the word processor when domestic duties called.

DJS

1 *Prelude*

Most people can identify half a dozen incidents which have been of particular significance to them: the day they fell in love for the very first time, the day a parent died, the day they came across a book which has been important ever since, the day they were suddenly whisked into hospital for a life-saving operation. Some Christians would include the day, even the hour, when they were 'converted', when (to use John Wesley's expression) their hearts were 'strangely warmed', though I have to say that I have never known such a precise moment myself: rather, the process has been a very gradual one, lasting the whole of my life so far, and no doubt still continuing.

One of those formative times for me was when I first became aware of the fact that English Literature was not just a subject studied in order to get through an examination, but a living and vibrant tradition which spoke deeply to something within oneself, a something whose existence had not even been suspected. It was rather akin to the thrill you feel when you find that you are actually swimming or riding a bicycle all on your own. I suppose it is a kind of falling in love and, for me, it was an experience to be encountered with even greater intensity when I first came across the music of the great sixteenth-century masters of polyphony, Palestrina and Vittoria, Lassus and Tallis.

Another such seminal occasion was my first visit to one of our greater parish churches, the magnificent Priory at Christchurch, which was then in Hampshire and which has subsequently migrated across the county boundary into Dorset. I was at that time a theological student in Cambridge and two of us were sent there for a week or two on what would now be called a placement, but which was then known as a parish visit. For me it was a spellbinding experience and I knew intuitively that this was one of those places, so aptly described in T. S. Eliot's phrase, 'where prayer has been valid'. On a more earthly level, it is a superb piece of architecture where, from one particular viewpoint, one can see examples of every style of English ecclesiastical architecture from Norman to Victorian, by way of Early English, Decorated, Perpendicular and Tudor.

Now each of these experiences, by and large, was not what most people would call a 'religious' experience: after all, there is very little that is overtly religious in the words of Graham Greene's novel, *The Heart of the Matter*, in the words of *Spem in Alium* by Thomas Tallis, or in the way in which stones and glass are arranged in an old building. Yet I believe that it is possible for experiences such as these to transcend the realm which we call 'mental' and to move into the dimension which many would describe as 'spiritual'.

Is there, though, such a sharp divide between the 'sacred' and the 'secular', or have we become conditioned since medieval times into believing that they occupy adjacent but independent territories, with guardposts and barbed wire between them? In attempting to answer that question, this book also goes well beyond it, because it explores how it is possible for human beings to know God, and not just to know him in the more conventional and obvious ways of prayer and sacrament, scripture and theology. Its primary aim is to point the way to a deeper knowledge and understanding of God through various other media, especially literature and music, art and architecture.

Perhaps I should explain at this point **how** the book came to be written in the first place. In recent years, I have slowly become aware that much of my life has been spent, consciously or otherwise, in trying to respond to the question which Jesus put to his disciples at Caesarea Philippi, 'Who do you say that I am?' (St Luke 9.20). Their immediate response to his previous question, 'Who do the people say that I am?' shows a good deal of confusion: some believed him to be a resurrected John the Baptist, others thought that he could be Elijah or one of the prophets of old, again mysteriously come to life.

It is Peter who provides the answer: 'You are the Christ of God'. It is not a response shared by everyone and there is no reason to feel guilty if after due reflection one comes up with a different one. Yet I believe that the honest attempt to come to a decision about Jesus is absolutely central to our life, since everything else ultimately depends on it.

My own response has taken me in a specific direction, first into membership of the Church of England and subsequently into its ordained ministry. There, for more than thirty-five years, I have read and re-read the Scriptures, both as part of the Daily Office of the Church and to nourish my own private devotion. In the Gospel according to Saint John, one of the recurring themes is that of blindness and sight: chapter 9, for instance, is devoted entirely to the story of a man born blind, to whom Jesus gives sight. Lately, when I have read this Gospel, I have been struck more than ever before by such phrases as 'Come and see' and 'Unless I see'. Here are four examples:

St John 1.18: **'No one has ever seen God; the only Son, who is in the bosom of the Father, he has made him known'.** This is the evangelist's own comment at the end of his Prologue to the Gospel. Having written some of the most profound words ever to come from the human pen, in which he develops his theology of Jesus as the eternal Word of God (St John 1.1–14), he concludes this opening section with the thought that the unseen and unseeable God has now been made known through his only Son, Jesus Christ. Greeks and Jews agreed that God was both invisible and unknowable, yet John's affirmation attests to the uniqueness of the self-revelation of the Father through his Son. We should be clear, however, that the author of the fourth Gospel is not in any way suggesting that human beings can have access to a vision of God in himself. It is the *principle* of the incarnation which he stresses in the Prologue, and expresses with matchless economy of words in that fundamentally important phrase, 'the Word became flesh'.

St John 1.39: **'Come and see'.** The context in which these words are spoken is almost unbelievably mundane. John the Baptist is standing with two of his disciples when Jesus passes by. 'Behold, the lamb of God!', he declares, and their immediate reaction is to follow Jesus and ask him where he is staying, to which Jesus replies with the words, 'Come and see'. The author even pinpoints the time of day as 'about the tenth hour', i.e. four o'clock in the afternoon. It is more than likely that this is a personal recollection of John the Evangelist, who may himself have been one of the two men. For me, the special significance of these words is the total openness of the invitation, an offer which is made not solely to the two who first accepted it but also to anyone else who is willing to respond.

St John 12.21: **'We wish to see Jesus'.** These words are addressed to the apostle Philip by a party of Greeks who have gone up to Jerusalem for the Passover Feast. It was a characteristic of the Greeks at this time to be enquirers into all things philo-sophical and theological, such was their desire to seek the truth, wherever it was to be found. We have no certain way of knowing why it was to Philip that they put their request, though it is an interesting fact that he and Andrew are the only ones among the Twelve with Greek names and it is to Andrew whom Philip turns for assistance! Whatever we may speculate, the reality is that those Greeks want to meet Jesus: their words also express the inner desire of the Christian to do the same, and at the same time the inner questioning as to whether such sight is possible.

St John 20.25: **'Unless I see'**. On the evening of the first Easter Day, the risen Lord had appeared to the disciples. Thomas, who was absent when this occurred, subsequently returned and spoke the words which have caused him to be branded as 'Doubting Thomas': 'Unless I see in his hands the print of the nails, and place my finger in the mark of the nails, I will not believe'. His demand for proof of Christ's resurrection accords very much with our own yearning for certainty: a week later, when his longing to see Jesus had been satisfied, his immediate response was to say, 'My Lord and my God!' (St John 20.28). How fortunate for Thomas, we may think, but we should then pause and listen carefully to our Lord's reply: 'Have you believed because you have seen me? Blessed are those who have not seen and yet believe.'

So how is it possible today for us to see Jesus and to know God? The answer to this apparently straightforward question is a good deal less easy to arrive at than we might at first suppose. Even though this book is about a vital and exciting personal journey, a journey available to everyone, our exploration will inevitably take us into the realms of theology and philosophy. During the course of it, we will come across a number of words which may not be familiar to all readers. Here are five of them, each with an uncom-plicated definition.

Aesthetics: the philosophy of taste or of the perception of beauty.
Epistemology: the theory of the method or grounds of know-
   ledge.
Liturgy: the study of worship.
Philosophy: the love, study or pursuit of wisdom.
Theology: the study or science which treats of God.

Using some of that specialised language, we can say that this book will examine the theological relationship between epistemology and aesthetics. In other words it is about knowing God, and knowing him especially through what we describe as things of beauty.

It will not be long before we discover that we soon run out of words that can adequately be used to describe God: hence the title of this book, *When Words Fail*. That is the point where signs and symbols, images and sounds, pictures and dreams, have to take over.

Those who have for long struggled to comprehend God through the use of the mind which God has given them often discover that, worthwhile as the attempt has been, it is doomed to failure. They are then able to let go of the unbearable tension of fighting a battle that cannot be won and allow God to draw them to himself, more through the heart than through the mind. This does not excuse us from coming to terms with all the fascinating intellectual problems that theology constantly poses, nor from remembering that part of our knowing God is to bring our minds to bear on the experiences of our senses and emotions.

F. C. Happold, in a book on meditation, has an apt quotation from St Bernard. When asked the question, 'What is God?', Bernard replied that the only answer he could give was 'He who is'. Happold continues:

> It is not possible to "think" about God, all that one can think about is some idea or image of God. For God is the Inexpressible, the Unknowable, the Ultimate Reality, the One "before whom all words recoil".[1]

It seems to have been the common experience of Christians down the ages, from Thomas the Apostle to Teilhard de Chardin, by way of Augustine and Aquinas, that **some** kind of sight is an essential ingredient in our pursuit of the knowledge of God. This statement is in no way inconsistent with those words of Christ, 'Blessed are those who have not seen and yet believe'. Except for the rare people who have received some special manifestation of Christ's presence, the normal Christian experience is one of seeing and knowing through some inner eye of faith.

An interesting question which I want to address in this book is the habit of chopping up the various activities of the mind into separate slices. It may be helpful at times to focus on our intellect, or our will, or our conscience, or our memory, or our fantasies, but the mind is really like the Psalmist's vision of Jerusalem, 'a city which is bound firmly together'. Of course, there are times when the mind suffers a partial or total collapse of its integrity – a *dis*integration – but I believe it to be much more helpful to think of it as having what Coverdale's version of the same Psalm calls 'a unity in itself' (Psalm 122.3).

That view is also reflected in my choice of approach to the themes of knowledge and beauty. It would have been possible, certainly tidier, and in some respects more usefully systematic, to have had separate chapters on such matters as Art, Liturgy, Music, Scripture, Science, Prayer, Ethics, Literature, and so on. This, though, would be to attempt to divide the indivisible and it explains why I have chosen to interweave those various threads in a more thematic approach.

There is, of course, a certain artificiality in making every chapter heading start with the same letter of the alphabet, yet when I first sketched out the areas I wanted to cover, those P-words kept on surfacing, and each of them is relevant to this study. The perceptive reader will also observe that I have occasionally strayed from the theme of a chapter in order to incorporate other ideas which, if slightly peripheral, are nevertheless relevant to the overall concept. I hope that each such excursion will be understood as acting as a commentary on the subject in hand, allowing it to be approached occasionally from an oblique angle.

⋆　⋆　⋆

Earlier in this chapter we looked at an incident which involved the apostle Philip. Here is another:

> Philip said to him, "Lord, show us the Father, and we shall be satisfied". Jesus said to him, "Have I been with you so long, and yet you do not know me, Philip? He who has seen me has seen the Father; how can you say, Show us the Father? Do you not believe that I am in the Father and the Father in me?" (St John 14.8–10)

The request, 'Show us the Father', is a wholly natural and understandable one, yet the reply of Jesus indicates both to Philip and to ourselves how spiritually unperceptive we are, for the truth is that when we see Jesus, we see God.

Edward Caswall's translation of a twelfth-century hymn contains these verses:

> O hope of every contrite heart,
> O joy of all the meek,
> **To those who ask how kind thou art,**
> **How good to those who seek!**
>
> **But what to those who find? Ah, this**
> **Nor tongue nor pen can show;**
> The love of Jesus, what it is
> None but his loved ones know.

The lines in bold print remind us that the search for God is a lifetime's work, if we are willing to allow it to become so, as we explore in ever greater depth the mysterious interaction between ourselves and our Lord. It is unwise to convince ourselves that there is no need to look any further because we have already found Jesus. There may be times when the going seems easy and the rewards obvious: it will not always be so, and we have to put a great deal into it if the search is to yield the best possible results:

> no other investigation that we ever undertake makes so heavy a demand upon our spiritual powers or requires for its successful conduct so mature and many-sided a wisdom as does our attempt to understand the relations of God to the soul.[2]

2 *Panorama*

The details of a spectacular sunrise in Brittany have stayed vividly in my mind for several years. It was heralded for over half an hour by a succession of changing colours on a bank of clouds and by the gradual hardening of the silhouette of the distant hills above which it had begun to climb. Then a fiery red ball appeared in the eastern sky, slowly growing from a tiny slither to a complete globe, the whole scene being immeasurably enhanced by the gentle mist rising from the water of the River Aulne in the immediate foreground.

Whenever I experience an occasion such as this, the opening words of the Prayer Book version of Psalm 19 invariably leap into my mind: 'The heavens declare the glory of God: and the firmament sheweth his handiwork'. A similar sense of the sheer glory of creation comes upon me when I see something which town dwellers seldom see, a sky full of stars on a dark night in the Dorsetshire countryside. I know of no better description than the one near the start of Thomas Hardy's novel, *Far from the Madding Crowd*. Gabriel Oak, a farmer, is inside his shepherd's hut on Norcome Hill, 'not far from lonely Toller Down', and it is nearly midnight on the eve of St Thomas's Day, the shortest day of the year:

> The sky was clear – remarkably clear – and the twinkling of all the stars seemed to be but throbs of one body, timed by a common pulse. The North Star was directly in the wind's eye, and since evening the Bear had swung round it outwardly to the east, till he was now at a right angle with the meridian. A difference of colour in the stars – oftener read of than seen in England – was really perceptible here. The sovereign brilliancy of Sirius pierced the eye with a steely glitter, the star called Capella was yellow, Aldebaran and Betelgueux shone with a fiery red.

From the available evidence, Hardy seems to have had an ambivalent attitude towards God, so it is difficult to know to what extent he himself interpreted such a sight as a manifestation of God's handiwork. As Stephen Platten has reminded us, he was unable to cast off religion completely and appears to have lived with an uncertainty about the created order, in which the 'regular heartbeat of the natural world vied with the cruelty of country life'.[1]

It would be a rare person indeed who did not have a tale to tell of one of the glories of the natural world, be it the distant view from a much-loved piece of high ground, the intricate and infinitely varied patterns of frost on a wintry window, or the wondrous beauty and simplicity of a rose. It is possible to argue that there must be a Creator behind all this: it is quite another thing to prove it, as generations of philosophers and theologians have discovered. No amount of purely intellectual argument will convince one that this is so, because the knowledge that we believe we have in these instances is not susceptible to proof by normal methods of verification. Proof, though, will be unnecessary if these signs speak to us of the existence of God, however tenuous our understanding of God may be.

Even the Bible refuses to give us the kind of help that we would find useful and authoritative. Certainly it lists some of the attributes of God: he is Almighty, Creator, Sovereign Lord. It tells us that God described himself to Moses as 'I am who I am', a phrase which the translators tell us can equally well be rendered as 'I will be what I will be' (Exodus 3.14). The Bible also tells us that he is the 'Alpha and the Omega, who is and who was and who is to come, the Almighty' (Revelation 1.8). Nowhere, however, does it give a description of God which will completely satisfy the philosopher or the theologian.

One of the challenges of the Bible is to force us to make up our own minds about God. Most of us are aware how much easier it is to clothe ourselves with ready-made, off-the-peg ideas, the views of other people, but these are seldom of real help in enabling us to come to our own decision and to establish our own sense of direction. We can begin the next stage of our pilgrimage only from the point where we are now and not from where someone else is or even where we think we ought to be.

There are two passages in particular which bring home to me the different ways in which God has revealed himself to human beings, to flesh and blood people such as we are ourselves. These revelations were given respectively to Moses and Elijah, when God appeared in a form which made him at least recognisable as God, though not necessarily in some material way. So awe-inspiring would be the full vision of the living God that Moses is told that he cannot see the face of God, but only his back:

> The Lord said to Moses "This very thing that you have spoken I will do; for you have found favour in my sight, and I know you by name." Moses said, "I pray thee, show me thy glory." And he said, "I will make all my goodness pass before you, and will proclaim before you my name The LORD; and I will be gracious to whom I will be gracious, and will show mercy on whom I will show mercy. But," he said, "you cannot see my face; for man shall not see me and live." And the Lord said, "Behold, there is a place by me where you shall stand upon the rock; and while my glory passes by I will put you in a cleft of the rock, and I will cover you with my hand until I have passed by; then I will take away my hand, and you shall see my back; but my face shall not be seen." (Exodus 33.17–23)

With Elijah, too, it was not possible to see the full glory of the Lord, though the wind, the earthquake and the fire must have seemed a terrifying manifestation of the all-powerful God. As the prophet was soon to discover, the presence which communicated itself to him was in none of these, but in what came after them:

> Elijah came to a cave and lodged there; and behold, the word of the Lord came to him, and he said to him, "What are you doing here, Elijah?" He said, "I have been very jealous for the Lord, the God of hosts; for the people of Israel have forsaken thy covenant, thrown down thy altars, and slain thy prophets with the sword; and I, even I only, am left; and they seek my life, to take it away." And he said, "Go forth, and stand upon the mount before the Lord." And behold, the Lord passed by, and a great and strong wind rent the mountains, and broke in pieces the rocks before the Lord, but the Lord was not in the wind; and after the wind an earthquake, but the Lord was not in the earthquake; and after the earthquake a fire, but the Lord was not in the fire; and after the fire a still small voice. (1 Kings 19.9–12)

There is all the world of difference between on the one hand these passing appearances of God and on the other his incarnation in Jesus Christ, for in the latter there is a *permanent* union between the fulness of God and the fulness of humanity. Ever since the days in which Jesus lived his earthly life, people have claimed, and still claim today, to know God through his incarnation. In what sense, we have to ask, is such knowledge possible? Might it not just be a matter of Freudian wish-fulfilment? The philosopher provides us with the beginnings of an answer, through the identification of three main kinds of knowledge. Anthony Flew describes them as:

(a) **Knowledge that**, or 'factual knowledge'.

(b) **Knowledge how**, or 'practical knowledge'.

(c) **Knowledge of**, (people, places, things), or 'knowledge by acquaintance'.[2]

However, as we shall see in a later chapter, there are other possible ways of knowing, which would not be acceptable to all philosophers, for example through the insights of mysticism. In terms of Flew's categories, we can have neither factual nor practical knowledge of God, *per se*, so this narrows it down to the third possibility, that is to say, knowledge by acquaintance.

One of the theological implications of this understanding of epistemology is that we cannot simply state that such and such is true about God, without giving any grounds for our assertion, nor will it be sufficient to fall back on such well-worn formulae as 'the Bible says' or 'the Church teaches'.

As a supremely positive aid to our approach to God, the Church provides us with the Liturgy, those acts of public worship, primarily the Eucharist (the service of Holy Communion). Christians believe that through them the human spirit is lifted towards the presence of God and that in them both the beauty of God's holiness and the holiness of God's beauty make known the reality of his presence among his people. This holds true whether the offering of worship is a plain, simple and unadorned prayer meeting in a plain, simple and unadorned building or whether it is a complex and sumptuous High Mass in a richly decorated baroque cathedral.

The Anglican liturgy, the one with which I am most familiar, is capable of enormous variety, but whenever it is presented imaginatively it can become, in the most intense way, the meeting point between the triangle which comprises God, ourselves, and those things which are aesthetically right. Many things contribute to this encounter:

music, such as settings of the Eucharist, anthems and hymns;

colour, in glass and vestments, stone and wood;

light, whether in a well-designed electrical installation or by the use of candles;

architecture, through which the very shape of the building speaks to us;

words, which when crafted with the skill of a poet have tremendous potency;

symbols and images, such as a cross, an icon, a statue or a painting;

metal, for example the silver or gold of a beautifully made chalice;

smell, most obviously that of incense, but not forgetting that ecclesiastical mustiness which for some is the very odour of sanctity;

silence, a commodity which by its very scarcity in daily life has a special impact liturgically.

It is incidentally worth remarking that those who lead the monastic life have much to teach us of the creative value of silence.

All these things, and the way they influence our bodies, can assist the process of making our minds and souls more open to God: when perceived in the particular context of the liturgy, they are transfigured by the light of Christ.

*   *   *

Most readers of this book will probably have their own favourite passages of scripture, among which will figure such pieces as the Creation story at the start of Genesis, the Shepherd psalm (Psalm 23), the Beatitudes (St Matthew 5.1–12) and St Paul's Hymn of Love (1 Corinthians 13). High on my own list comes the Emmaus story in St Luke 24.13–36, in which Jesus gradually reveals himself to two people, Cleopas and his companion (wife? friend?) and does it in no fewer than three separate ways, each of which reflects that transforming and transfiguring power of the presence of Christ.

First, he reveals himself on the journey by opening their eyes to all the things in their scriptures (those which we now call the Old Testament) that point to himself. Next, he reveals himself at their own dining table in what is clearly a eucharistic act: 'He took the bread and blessed and broke it, and gave it to them'. Was there something characteristic in this gesture that caused their eyes to be opened or was it perhaps at this point that they noticed his hands, hands which only 48 hours earlier had been nailed to the cross? Thirdly, he reveals himself when they have returned post-haste to Jerusalem to report their extraordinary encounter to the other disciples, this time making himself known through the assembly of his faithful people.

So through Word and Sacrament and Fellowship, the risen Lord is **made known** to his disciples of old. It is in precisely the same ways that he is **made known** to his disciples of today, as all these three elements combine in the liturgy of the Church.

In common with the story of the Last Supper, this particular event has been an inspiration to artists for many centuries. Probably the best-known painting of it is Rembrandt's 'The Pilgrims at Emmaus', dating from 1648. Seated at a table which has on it both an overthrow and a white cloth are three men. It is the moment of recognition: the man on the left holds his hand to his mouth in amazement while his companion to the right gazes spellbound at Jesus who is in the centre, behind the table and facing the viewer. His hands are breaking the bread and a mystical light surrounds his head. The arrival through a door to the right of a servant bringing in more food on a plate heightens the impact of the event by bringing it into the 'everyday of life'.

Unlike certain incidents recorded in the Gospels, which are made special by their very ordinariness, so much religious art actually makes the event other-wordly and thus removes it from our range of experience. Giotto and Stanley Spencer alike, though separated by enormous chasms of time and culture, possess the gift of making something special out of the ordinariness of life. In this way, it transcends the ordinary so that the ordinary becomes sacramental. Much of today's television reportage has precisely the opposite effect, because it trivialises everything by trying to make it extraordinary.

My brief description of the work by Rembrandt fails to do justice to the original work: even the attempt to describe it leads us speedily towards the point from which this book takes its title, *when words fail*. A careful examination of the masterpiece in the Louvre, or a good reproduction, demonstrates the power of a work of art to bring us closer to God, not simply because it has a religious subject but because it is itself a thing of beauty, something capable of transmitting aesthetic pleasure.

Donald Whittle has tried to clarify the intricate relationship between art and faith and in particular the complex nature of the interaction of the three principal components, the artist, his own beliefs and his work. Whilst emphasising the danger of generalisations, especially in the field of aesthetics, he has sought to distinguish Christian art from any other art, a differentiation with which not all Christians will necessarily agree:

> 1. "Christian art" can be regarded as an historical category. The term would then apply only to those works whose thematic material is overtly Christian – paintings of Biblical scenes, musical settings of religious texts, figures of Biblical characters, and literature dealing with the main themes of Christian belief.
> 2. The term can also be used in a wider sense as indicating some connection between a work of art and a Christian vision and understanding of the world. Some novels, plays, paintings, etc., may be said to share in the Christian vision even if they have no explicit Christian references.
> 3. We can also define Christian art as a re-enactment of creation. In this case, all works of art, whatever their subject matter and whatever the attitude of the artist, can be seen as sheer imaginative works of creation, and as such, reflections on the conviction that God created man to be, in his own turn, a creator.[3]

It would not be difficult to criticise the third definition as a denial of the continuity of God's creative act since the artist does not 're-enact', but permits himself or herself to be an instrument of that creative energy. Conversely, the artist can also become the instrument of those negative forces which Jesus referred to as 'the prince of darkness'.

It is at this point that I would like to examine in more detail what we mean by art. Whereas the 'fine arts' are properly limited to painting, architecture and sculpture, 'the arts' covers a far wider field, including music, poetry, photography, television, the cinema, dance, dramatic art and now, one would presumably have to add, the art of the hologram. Anyone who has ever tried to define art will know how difficult it is to arrive at a satisfactory answer. To ask the question, 'What is art?', is an excellent way of starting a lively discussion among philosophers, art critics, art historians and, of course, artists themselves. This is hardly surprising when one realises how different cultures at different stages of their development have looked at art in a variety of ways: the caveman at Lascaux had a very different social agenda from that of his later compatriot, the French impressionist! But art is not only a cerebral matter: to classify it as such would be to fail to take into account the question as to why some people are compelled to *make* art, sometimes (as with van Gogh) at terrible personal cost.

This is true for architecture as well. The cultural medium is a powerful determinant of the finished product, whether that be an Assyrian ziggurat, a Greek temple, a Roman amphitheatre, a Byzantine basilica, a Norman cathedral, a Tudor royal palace, a Georgian town house, a Victorian railway station or a 1960s shopping precinct. When it comes to specifically ecclesiastical architecture, the question that has to be asked over and over again is, 'What is it *for*?'. Another increasingly pertinent question for our time is, 'What are we going to do with it now that it is no longer needed for its original purpose?'. Simply because it is a church, and maybe not even an attractive church, must we at all costs preserve it? This raises an important aesthetic and theological issue, since our answers to such questions depend substantially on our view as to whether we can actually come to a knowledge of God through sacred places, or whether it is solely a matter of faith. To pose the dilemma in this way is perhaps to polarise it unnecessarily, for faith and buildings are not mutually exclusive. Wherever you see a church or chapel, you are seeing an act of faith in solid form, even though the time may have come when one has to say that the original intention of faith is no longer best served by the preservation of that particular structure, powerful as it may still be as an icon of God.

Images can be particularly helpful in nourishing the soul: we depend on them far more than we may be aware and this is as true in the realm of literature as it is in the world of art. There are many novels which, although they may not appear so at first sight, are essentially religious because they draw our attention to the basic condition of our humanity, a humanity created in the image of God and a humanity shared by God in the incarnate life of Jesus Christ. When you start writing about the 'human condition', if you are a good novelist you will populate your pages with real-life people living in real-life situations, but you will also deal in images

15

and symbols which will speak to the reader as no words on their own can speak. One twentieth-century writer who has done this consistently in all his novels over a long period of years is Sir William Golding (1911–1993). I commend his works to anyone who wants an illustration of what I have been saying. When you read *The Spire*, *Lord of the Flies* or *Rites of Passage*, you will find image after image, some of which will make you feel uncomfortable because you suddenly realise that you are looking at yourself, perhaps some aspect of yourself which you had never realised was there, and with which you now have to come to terms.

In the allied realm of poetry, where one of the basic components is the provision of disparate images, the writer paints miniatures in words to create a series of mental pictures which are designed to convey his ideas to our minds as vividly as possible. In so doing, the poet also seeks to convey sense impressions (texture, passion, melody) that provide the raw material from which we can create our own ideas. What power there is, for instance, in Dylan Thomas's economical use of words in *Under Milk Wood* where he describes the deep sea as 'Davy dark' or the moonless night as 'bible-black'.

There has been much poetry written in every generation, as there is today, which is specifically Christian. I have chosen almost at random half a dozen snatches which, while doing little justice to their contexts, illustrate a long tradition and may lead the reader to look for further examples.

George Herbert (1593–1633) has these words as the closing verse of his short poem, *The Agony*:

> Who knows not Love, let him assay
> And taste that juice, which on the cross a pike
> Did set again abroach; then let him say
> If ever he did taste the like.
> Love is that liquour sweet and most divine,
> Which my God feels as blood; but I, as wine.

In a mere fifty words, the poet confronts our imagination with an affecting picture of the love of God which, in the agony of crucifixion, feeds us on the wine of his blood. Not a noun is wasted: Love, juice, cross, pike, liquour, God, blood and wine, all play their part in building up the required image.

John Milton (1608–1674) puts into the mouth of the Chorus in *Samson Agonistes* these words:

> Just are the ways of God,
> And justifiable to men;
> Unless there be who think not God at all:
> If any be, they walk obscure;
> For of such doctrine never was there school,
> But the heart of the fool,
> And no man therein doctor but himself.

This time, in even fewer words, the author is writing a commentary in verse on the Psalmist's statement, 'The fool says in his heart, There is no God'. Quite apart from the skilful choice and crafting of the words used by the poet, what makes it so arresting is the way in which the reader is challenged to examine and to justify his or her own theological stance.

The nonconformist divine, **Philip Doddridge** (1702–1751), well-known as the author of many popular hymns such as 'O God of Bethel, by whose hand' and 'Hark the glad sound! the Saviour comes', wrote this brief poem:

> "Live while you live", the Epicure would say,
> "And seize the pleasures of the present day".
> "Live while you live", the sacred Preacher cries,
> "And give to God each moment as it flies".
> Lord, in my views let both united be;
> I live in pleasure, when I live in Thee.

Again, in just fifty words, so much is said with such wonderful economy of speech. Two views of pleasure are set against each other with, it would seem, a choice to be made between them. However, in the last couplet, the poet releases the tension by suggesting that the two views are not, after all, mutually exclusive: indeed, more than suggesting that they can merely co-exist, he is making the strong theological statement that God is the source of all pleasure.

Gerard Manley Hopkins (1844–1889), Jesuit priest, scholar, pastor and poet, is usually somewhat unrestrained in his use of rhythm, but these last six lines of his sonnet, *Patience, Hard Thing*, exhibit an almost uncharacteristic discipline:

17

> We hear our hearts grate on themselves: it kills
> To bruise them dearer. Yet the rebellious wills
> Of us we do bid God bend to him even so:
> And where is he who more and more distils
> Delicious kindness? – He is patient. Patience fills
> His crisp combs, and that comes those ways we know.

What is totally characteristic is his idiosyncratic use of words: it is not that the words themselves are at all unfamiliar but rather that they have been ordered in such a manner that we have to search for their hidden significance and then find in them such an intensity of feeling as to give an overall impression of deep devotion.

D. H. Lawrence (1885–1930), pantheist though he was, has these lines in *St Matthew*, doubtless influenced by his strong biblical upbringing in chapel and Sunday School:

> I, on the other hand,
> Am drawn to the Uplifted, as all men are drawn,
> To the Son of Man
> Filius Meus.

Lawrence did not greatly approve of the world or society in which he lived: how consciously, we may wonder, was he expressing a little of his own longing for something better when he tried to put himself into the shoes of the Evangelist?

And **John Betjeman** (1906–1984), in his *Verses turned in aid of A Public Subscription (1952) towards the restoration of the Church of St Katherine, Chiselhampton, Oxon* writes thus:

> On country mornings sharp and clear
> The penitent in faith draw near
> And kneeling here below
> Partake the Heavenly Banquet spread
> Of Sacramental Wine and Bread
> And JESUS' presence know.

The poetry may lack the exquisite wording of Herbert and the profundity of thought of Hopkins, yet it possesses a directness of expression that takes the reader to the eucharistic heart of the matter in a straightforward yet felicitous way, an effect which is skilfully achieved by the interplay of the adjectives and nouns which make up the greater part of it.

Among the twentieth-century poets, my favourites are T. S. Eliot and R. S. Thomas, and I shall have more to say about both of them later on. Because they speak about such profound matters as the relationship between time and eternity, and the ways in which the gap between ourselves and our God can be bridged, the *Four Quartets* of T. S. Eliot must rank among the highest reaches of devotional writing, even though this may not be readily apparent when one comes to them for the first time. The same is true of *Threshold*, *Pluperfect* and *Directions*, all of which are to be found in *Between Here and Now*, one of the many collections of poems by R. S. Thomas.

From Christopher Marlowe and William Shakespeare, through William Congreve and Richard Sheridan, to Samuel Beckett and Arthur Miller, the dramatists also address that 'human condition' from which we cannot escape: in doing so they speak of the God who has made us as we are.

★　★　★

Music, too, has a very special power to lift the human spirit to a deeper understanding of the mystery of God. There is about it something peculiarly appropriate which makes it the most fitting of all the art forms for use in public worship. It has an innate 'spirituality', a quality which will be explored in more detail and which illustrates perfectly the title of this book, since it is here for so many people that the pilgrim's journey is given a fresh momentum and a renewed impetus, at the point *when words fail*.

The psychiatrist Anthony Storr believes that it is not only professional musicians who consider music to be of the utmost significance among the varied experiences of life:

> Music exalts life, enhances life, and gives it meaning. Great music outlives the individual who created it. It is both personal and beyond the personal. For those who love it, it remains as a fixed point of reference in an unpredictable world. Music is a source of reconciliation, exhilaration, and hope which never fails.[4]

There was one particular era, at least in Britain, when religious experience and aesthetic sensibility went hand in hand. In a book

19

subtitled *Aesthetics and religion in Victorian literature*, Hilary Fraser draws our attention to the long history of religious patronage which has enabled the arts to flourish and to testify in themselves to the alliance between beauty and truth. More specifically she writes of the evocation of religious meaning in the nineteenth-century in these terms:

> In the visual arts, painters as diverse as the Pre-Raphaelite Holman Hunt and the spectacularly dramatic John Martin took as their subject-matter biblical scenes and invested their art with a peculiarly Victorian religious mysticism. Gothic Revival architecture exploited religious emotion in every soaring arch and pointed pinnacle. Quantities of religious poetry and novels were written. The influence of the arts upon Victorian religion were equally far-reaching. Aesthetic sensibility defined the special character of the Victorian Anglo-Catholic revival, and a new style of "literary" Catholicism developed among writers such as Coventry Patmore, Aubrey de Vere, Francis Thompson, the Wards and the Meynells ... Poetry came to be accepted by many as the most appropriate way of expressing religious truths, and as the key to the interpretation of Scriptural meaning.[5]

One of the problems which arises when we try to define beauty is a cultural one. Because beauty has different connotations in different cultures, the artist may be more fundamentally concerned with truth than with beauty, since truth has a wider cultural universality.

What in Victorian times seemed a natural alliance has now become for the great majority of people, if not a divorce, then at least a separation. To bring the 'things of God' and the 'things of beauty' together again into a living relationship is one of the most interesting and challenging tasks which will face the theologian and the aesthete in the twenty first-century.

Although the New Testament has little to say specifically about beauty (the word itself appears surprisingly infrequently) it could be that a fresh look at scripture may be the best launching pad for such an endeavour. It is all too easy, as we so often see, for the artist to debase the biblical coinage, whether in terms of architecture, music, scripture, painting or literature, yet it is totally within the power of the artist to create something which has exactly the opposite effect, to add almost beyond measure to the value of that scriptural coinage. The western church might do well to learn the art of painting icons, for that is far more than the representation of an image: it is in itself a form of prayer.

Prayer, of course, is where many people feel that they are on reasonably familiar territory: in some form or another, it has been the home ground of religious experience for as long as they can remember. Those who have been brought up in an atmosphere in which prayer is a natural part of living need to remember that this is no longer so for the majority, for whom their only experience has been at school assemblies (not always prayerfully conducted) and at the occasional wedding or carol service. As for **private** prayer, this is something only to be resorted to in emergencies, and even then with very little expectation of success, since other means have already failed. Yet it is here more than anywhere else in the spiritual life that one makes that communion with God which is so vital a part of our knowing him.

We do not need to have become extremely well-versed in the art of meditation and contemplation in order to begin to experience something of the reality of the presence of the God to whom we pray, as the totality of our personality becomes involved. Body, intellect, will and emotion each has its part to play in our response to him. In the language of epistemology, we not only 'know that', but we also simply 'know'.

3 *Pilgrimage*

John Bunyan's classic masterpiece, *The Pilgrim's Progress*, traces the journey of its central character, Christian, 'from this world to that which is to come'. His allegory of the human search for salvation reminds us that we are each involved in a personal journey, the end of which lies beyond this present life. The concept of pilgrimage has itself become a metaphor of the life of every Christian and is implicit in these words from the Epistle to the Hebrews:

> Here we have no lasting city, but we seek the city which is to come. (Hebrews 13.14)

The seventeenth-century English mystical poet, Henry Vaughan (1622–1695), turns this concept into a memorable poem:

> My soul, there is a country
> Far beyond the stars,
> Where stands a winged sentry
> All skilful in the wars.
>
> There above noise, and danger,
> Sweet peace sits crowned with smiles,
> And One born in a manger
> Commands the beauteous files.
>
> He is thy gracious Friend,
> And – O my soul, awake! –
> Did in pure love descend,
> To die here for thy sake.
>
> If thou canst get but thither,
> There grows the flower of peace,
> The Rose that cannot wither,
> Thy fortress and thy ease.
>
> Leave then thy foolish ranges,
> For none can thee secure
> But One who never changes,
> Thy God, thy life, thy cure.

God, then, is the journey's end and Jesus Christ is the companion on the way, as he was for those two people on the road to Emmaus. In this chapter, I want to explain how music, literature and the visual arts have accompanied me on my own pilgrimage, helping and encouraging me along the road by the glimpses they give of the beauty that awaits its full revelation beyond the gates of the celestial city.

As a teenager growing up in the south-western outskirts of London, I used to spend a lot of time on the North Downs: there were few Saturdays when, either alone or with friends, I was not somewhere in that part of Surrey on my bicycle. Between Guildford and Dorking, there are several points along the top of the scarp slope from which one can see miles away on the horizon the distant outline of the other extremity of the Weald, the South Downs, with the Tillingbourne valley, the wealden clays and sands, and the Vale of Sussex in between. Joining these various viewpoints is an ancient track known as the Pilgrims' Way, which stretches the entire distance from Winchester to Canterbury. When at the age of sixteen I entered the 6th-form of my school and was introduced for the first time to Chaucer, the Pilgrims' Way took on an entirely new dimension. As part of the English Literature syllabus for what was then called the Higher School Certificate (shortly afterwards to be replaced by A-level) we made the acquaintance of the great fourteenth century poet's *Canterbury Tales*. The opening words of the *Prologue* have been with me ever since:

> When that Aprille with his showres swoot
> The drought of Marche hath perced to the root,
> And bathed every veyn in suche licour,
> From which vertu engendred is the flour;
> When Zephirus eek with his swete breeth
> Enspired hath in every holte and heeth
> The tendre croppes, and the yonge sonne
> Hath in the Ram his halfe course runne,
> And smale fowles maken melodie
> That slepen al the night with open eye,
> So pricketh them nature in their corages:-
> Thenne longen folk to go on pilgrimages,
> And palmers for to seeken strange strandes,
> To distant seintes, known in sondry landes,

And specially, from every shires ende
Of Engelond, to Canterbury they wende,
The holy blisful martir for to seeke,
That them hath holpen when that they were weeke.[1]

A superb modern translation by Nevill Coghill appeared just a year too late to help me with my exams, though it was very good so soon after them to have a version in today's English. Needless to. say, much time was spent in reading the racier tales, which failed to find a place in the official syllabus, to the detriment of those portions which we were supposed to be studying! His rendering of those opening words goes like this:

When the sweet showers of April fall and shoot
Down through the drought of March to pierce the root,
Bathing every vein in liquid power
From which there springs the engendering of the flower,
When also Zephyrus with his sweet breath
Exhales an air in every grove and heath
Upon the tender shoots, and the young sun
His half-course in the sign of the *Ram* has run,
And the small fowl are making melody
That sleep away the night with open eye
(So nature pricks them and their heart engages)
Then people long to go on pilgrimages
And palmers long to seek the stranger strands
Of far-off saints, hallowed in sundry lands,
And specially, from every shire's end
In England, down to Canterbury they wend
To seek the holy blissful martyr, quick
In giving help to them when they were sick.[2]

Although Chaucer's pilgrims started their journey to Canterbury from London, one could so easily envisage a similar motley group making its way along the North Downs on their pilgrimage to the shrine of St Thomas Becket, whose murder in 1170 led to his being proclaimed a martyr a mere two years later.

T. S. Eliot reconstructs the scene masterfully in his play *Murder in the Cathedral*, written for the 1935 Canterbury Festival. Just before the arrival of the 'slightly tipsy' Knights who are to kill the Archbishop, the Priests call for the doors of the Cathedral to be barred against them. Thomas replies:

Unbar the door! throw open the doors!
I will not have the house of prayer, the church of Christ,
The sanctuary, turned into a fortress.
The Church still protects her own, in her own way, not
As oak and stone; stone and oak decay,
Give no stay, but the Church shall endure.
The Church shall be open, even to our enemies.
Open the door![3]

Although some of the set books were not ones I would have chosen to study, I subsequently came to realise that those last two years at school were an unbarring of the doors of the sanctuary of my mind and that they had laid the foundations for a lifetime's enjoyment of reading. What a wonderful awakening it was and how different it all seemed from anything that had gone before! Shakespeare we had done from our first year, starting with *The Tempest* and much of it simply passed me by at that stage. But now, suddenly, the whole wide world of literature opened out before me, not only the set books of Chaucer, Thackeray, Milton, Keats, Hardy and Shakespeare, but a host of others too. From then on, I cannot remember a time when I have been without at least one book on the go, a fact for which I am extremely grateful.

Some years before this, I began another aspect of my continuing pilgrimage of discovery when at the age of nine I joined the choir of the parish church of All Saints', Kingston-upon-Thames. There, two entirely new dimensions began to open up before me simultaneously, worship and music, and the two have seldom been far apart in my life ever since. Again, I am profoundly thankful for that and for the support they have given me for over half a century. It was at this stage that I was introduced to three kinds of music which still form the core of the Anglican repertoire.

First, the Psalms, and in particular that unique method of singing them known as the Anglican chant, with a melody line capable of almost infinite variation, serving as a vehicle for the words, which are 'pointed' accordingly, i.e. arranged in such a way that they are accommodated to the basic structure of the chant. Secondly, anthems, musical settings of words which are usually, though by no means exclusively, from scripture. The repertoire of such anthems, built up over a period of 500 years, is enormous and within it there is music for every occasion and every mood. Thirdly, there are the 'settings', musical arrangements of the traditional canticles of Morning and Evening Prayer (Matins and Evensong) and of the sung parts of the service of Holy Communion: here again the repertoire is colossal. The links in the chain of composition have held together unbroken throughout that period, despite – or sometimes because of – the succession of upheavals which have disturbed the life of the Church of England, notably the Reformation, the comings and goings of several versions of the Book of Common Prayer, the Commonwealth and the Restoration of the Monarchy, the Evangelical and Catholic Revivals, and those sad periods of spiritual stagnation which have afflicted the Church from time to time.

It was into this great heritage that I was plunged when the years of my age were still in single figures, at first with almost total bewilderment, but with growing mental, musical and spiritual comprehension. Fifteen years later, I was again bowled over by a different musical experience, when I heard the monks of Solesmes Abbey singing Vespers. In a mysterious and undefinable way, that music in that setting succeeded in conveying to me something of the quality of holiness: perhaps it was the realisation that Gregorian chant, in that particular context, was a perfect way of expressing the words of the Psalms. This feeling has been reinforced for me lately by spending several weeks among the monks of another Benedictine Abbey, that at Landévennec in Brittany, and sharing with them in the singing of the Daily Office, both in its Gregorian and modern forms.

The church in which I sang as a boy was affiliated to what was then called the School of English Church Music (now the Royal School of Church Music) and I gradually came to learn not just the meaning, but also the significance, of its motto, *Psallam spiritu et mente*: 'I will sing with the spirit and with the understanding also'. Slowly the message got through that the real purpose was not just to enjoy a good sing but that the worship should be adorned with a particular kind of beauty. It was not until much later in life that I began to understand that what we were actually doing in these services was to make a response to God from the deep resources which he himself had placed within us. Only as adults, I suspect, do we see the offering of worship as the offering of our entire being, just as the offering of bread and wine at the Eucharist is symbolic of the offering of everything we have and all that we are. There are two poems which express this in a way which I find peculiarly appropriate. The first is by the Victorian writer, Horatius Bonar, and it contains this verse:

Not for the lip of praise alone
Nor e'en the praising heart,
I ask, but for a life made up
Of praise in every part.

The second, by George Herbert, has these lines:

Seven whole days, not one in seven,
I will praise thee;
In my heart, though not in heaven,
I can raise thee.
Small it is, in this poor sort
To enrol thee:
E'en eternity's too short
To extol thee.

Again, I believe that it is only our adult understanding that enables us to realise that, whilst our imagination is hard at work in all these experiences of music and in our participation in the liturgy, there is no separate part of our being labelled 'religious imagination'. It is rather that this aspect of our imaginative processes is the culmination of all the others, and not something which is limited merely to cerebral activity: the strings of our hearts are also being plucked.

Possibly the first glimpses of this came to me when I saw a cathedral for the first time. By now I was twelve and a Second World War evacuee in North Devon at the time of the Flying Bombs, the V1s. I was fortunate enough to have been billetted with the Mayor of Great Torrington who, because he was also a member of Devon County Council, had an extra petrol ration to enable him to attend meetings in Exeter. One day he took me along for the ride and let me loose on the city. Before long I had discovered the Cathedral, which was quite the largest building I had ever been in and in every way the grandest.

In the intervening years I have visited the majority of our cathedrals and have been impressed by something in every one of them, be it Salisbury's spire, Ely's lantern, Coventry's windows, Winchester's nave or the sheer grandeur of Durham. But it is Exeter which remains as the prototypical impression of space, dignity, beauty and mystery. What I was not aware of at the time, at least what I certainly could not have verbalised, was the quite intense mixture of emotions which I was experiencing, including wonder, reverence, awe, and even fear.

Not long ago I paid my first visit to the two cathedrals in Liverpool and felt much the same set of emotions, with even now a touch of fear at the enormous scale of the Anglican building. It is true that not everybody reacts in the same way as I did or still do: some will find the architecture of this or that church or cathedral aesthetically satisfying but will not be swept by the same feelings of awe. For others, such emotional reactions will be very much more intense than mine. Thus it always is with an aesthetic experience. What for one person is a sensational musical performance will leave another unmoved; what may leave me cold in the world of painting will give another person a very special feeling of pleasure.

What looks 'just right' in art or architecture or sculpture prob- ably is right, though this is admittedly a subjective way of approaching it and will not satisfy those who demand a more objective set of criteria. We do well to listen to those with a more highly-developed aesthetic sense than our own, noting carefully what they say about the rightness or wrongness of things, yet the ultimate question is, 'Does it satisfy me?' I used to see Stonehenge nearly every day for twenty months of my military service and in those days you could walk right up to it, touch it, and stand beneath the great trilithons: to me it looked as right as the spire of Salisbury Cathedral eight miles away.

As a schoolboy on my first visit to France, I saw the famous glass of Chartres Cathedral and knew that it was as right in its own way as the architecture of the chateau at Azay-le-Rideau nearly 100 miles away. A few years ago I saw the Book of Kells in the library of Trinity College, Dublin and I knew that it was as right in its own way as the architecture of the Palace at Hampton Court. Two decades ago I saw the exterior of Beverley Minster in Yorkshire and knew again that it was as right as the interior of Romsey Abbey in Hampshire. The reader could no doubt produce a similar list, though we should all be aware that in making our judgements they are not solely a matter of intellectual assessment: all sorts of other factors are at work as well, physical, emotional, psychological and spiritual.

The artist might express this sense of rightness by saying that only when the painting speaks to him or her does it appear to have reached the point of being just right. In other words, there comes a paradoxical moment at which the work has more to say to the artist than he or she has put into it.

To return to my younger days, my next incursion into the world of books came when I was 18 and had three months to fill in between leaving school and being called up for National Service. It had been suggested at that time that I might consider a career as a librarian, so I spent those weeks as an assistant in the headquarters of Surrey County Library. Although I was on occasions reprimanded for reading books instead of cataloguing them, it did give me a very much wider insight into the literary world. Whereas the school library had measured its volumes in hundreds, and the local public library in thousands, here were books in their tens of thousands. Access to this astonishing array of fiction, non-fiction and reference books turned out to be an excellent preparation for subsequent study in university libraries.

During the early months of military training there was practically no time for any kind of reading at all, with the day fully regulated from well before dawn to long after dusk: the only book I can remember reading during the weeks of basic training was the New Testament, a tiny copy of which I had been given by my parish priest a day or two before joining up. This, to the barely-concealed amusement of my fellow squaddies, I would read last thing at night and it began to dawn on me how much of the teaching of Jesus (for it was from the Gospels that I read mostly) was concerned with demonstrating that the most mundane objects of normal daily life have something to show us of God. It was as if he were saying, 'If you want to know God, then start by thinking of this lamp, this lily, this gate, this sheep, that sower, that tree, that net, that coin: start with some image which you can see clearly and work on from there'.

Forty years later, when reading *Fifth Business*, which is Part One of Robertson Davies's splendid *Deptford Trilogy*, I came across a passage which immediately set up all sorts of abreactive reverberations. Dunstan Ramsey, the hero of the story, has lied about his age and is now in the Canadian army in World War I: he happens to possess a New Testament, which he reads avidly because he loves books and that is the only one he has with him:

This gained me a disagreeable reputation as a religious fellow, a Holy Joe, and even the chaplain avoided that kind, for they were sure trouble, one way or another. My nickname was Deacon, because of my *Testament* reading. It was useless to explain that I read it not from zeal but curiosity and that long passages of it confirmed my early impression that religion and *Arabian Nights* were true in the same way. (Later I was able to say that they were both psychologically rather than literally true, and that psychological truth was really as important in its own way as historical verification; but while I was a young soldier I had no vocabulary for such argument, though I sensed the truth of it.)[4]

In the years immediately following, first at the University of Birmingham, where I read Geography but lived as an ordinand 'hosteller' in the Queen's Theological College, and then at Westcott House, one of the two Anglican Theological Colleges in Cambridge, I began to get to grips with the whole question of religious language, knowledge and verification.

For me, one of the most interesting areas of study was the Old Testament, which involved assessing the internal evidence concerning the way in which God was known to people in those days and in that part of the world. It soon became apparent that one mode for the manifestation of this knowledge was in the recognition by the people of Israel of God's lordship not only over themselves but over all the world. The symbol of this relationship with God was the Covenant, a two-way contract which required on their part a response of love, as well as one of obedience. In a passage which was subsequently to be quoted by Jesus, the commitment was made clear:

Hear, O Israel: The Lord our God is one Lord; and you shall love the Lord your God with all your heart, and with all your soul, and with all your might. (Deuteronomy 6.4–5)

Because of their particular understanding of the Covenant relationship, the Israelites did come to a knowledge of God, not all at once, but slowly over a period of many centuries. Then, with the incarnation, for which so much of Jewish religious history had been a preparation, it became possible to know God in the fullest way, through Jesus Christ. One of the tasks of the theologian today is to try to unfold all this, to come to a deeper understanding of it himself or herself, and then to communicate it to the rest of us. It is said that a university is a place to which you go to learn more and more about less and less: this is particularly true in departments of theology and philosophy, so much so that it sometimes leads to a situation where God is virtually eliminated because no one is any longer sure of what can be known or said about him!

One of the best contemporary interpreters of the Christian faith is the German theologian, Hans Küng, who addresses the whole question of the existence of God in his great tomes, *On Being a Christian* and *Does God Exist?* in which he argues that we must first bring an attitude of fundamental trust and basic confidence to the reality of our own existence. He maintains that people express what they understand by God in different ways:

> The mysterious and unshakable ground of what is – despite everything – a meaningful life, the center [*sic*] and depth of man, of human fellowship, of reality as a whole; the final, supreme authority on which everything depends.[5]

He concedes, though, that it is possible to deny God: 'If someone says that there is no God, his claim cannot be positively refuted'. Here once again we come up against the difficulty of making statements about God which will be meaningful to the philosopher, who may allege that they cannot be verified. This places the onus on the theologian to make as clear as possible what he means when he uses such a word as 'God'. Although we may not ourselves be philosophers, we cannot simply ignore the philosophical implications either of the existence of God or of our ability to know him, which are central to this book and to which we will return more than once.

Following my ordination in York Minster, and serving as a curate in parishes as widely separated as Yorkshire and Hampshire, I found that the demands of parochial work and of a young family sidelined some of my preoccupations, but music and literature remained a constant source of pleasure and a stimulus to mind and soul. I found myself reading the works of Christian writers such as Graham Greene, Charles Williams, Morris West and C. S. Lewis, and also making my first inroads into the great Russian novelists, Tolstoy and Dostoyevsky, who have a way of treating the 'human predicament' on the grand scale. Another real joy was to discover writers from across the Atlantic, such as Steinbeck and Harper Lee, who again use the novel (much as Dickens did) to throw into clearer relief the problems of contemporary life.

It was not until I became the incumbent of a parish that I had to take personal initiatives concerning church buildings. Up to that point, they were part of the givenness of the situation. Now I had to address myself to the problems and opportunities which they presented and to share with others, who would be there long after I left, both the well-being of the fabric and the equally pressing question of how best to adapt ancient buildings to modern requirements, especially liturgical ones.

Much emphasis was placed at that time on the need to focus the liturgy on a central altar, where this was physically possible, and a valuable shift of emphasis it was. As the Church of England experimented with its new forms of service for the principal act of worship, the Eucharist, so the understanding of what was being done, and by whom and for whom, was also changing. The new emphasis was not on the back view of a priest in the remote distance with a congregation allowed to participate infrequently during the service. Instead, the whole people of God gathered round the altar, if not literally then at least symbolically, and together offered 'the sacrifice of praise and thanksgiving'. Needless to say, not everyone found this either a helpful shift of emphasis or aesthetically satisfying.

The church building itself and its internal layout are strong influences in our personal and corporate spirituality. As a geographer, I was trained to understand the importance of 'place' and the profound influence which our surroundings exert on the nature and quality of our lives. When it comes to the spiritual content of those lives, insofar as that can be detached from the remainder, the same influences prevail and we are worked upon by all sorts of signals, whether or not we are aware of our perception of them, signals emanating from and transmitted by the building itself and all that it contains. Therefore, what we do in our worship needs to be complemented by the surroundings, wherever this is practicable, to enable us to respond to the *Sursum Corda*, 'Lift up your hearts: we lift them to the Lord'.

Part of this 'lifting up' is the raising of our imagination: art in all its forms helps to do this, though it is inseparable from life as a whole. It is sometimes said that whereas the normal furnishings of a church all have a useful function to fulfil (altar, font, pulpit, organ), works of art such as paintings and sculpture serve no useful purpose in practice. This may be so, but purely practical considerations should not be the final arbiter of worth: what these works can do, which a pew or a lectern may not do, is to allow the imagination to ponder the subject and to find in it a value which is not intrinsic to the object itself. This, of course, is not to deny the artistic worth of, say, the great carved brass lecterns and splendid stone pulpits which are to be found in many a church or cathedral. The significance of sculpture in this respect is not the same as that of painting because the particular visual impact of a three-dimensional object is very different from that of a flat surface. As so much sculpture is concerned with the human body, we need not be surprised to find in our churches many representations of Christ, the Blessed Virgin Mary and the Saints, whether seen in isolation or as part of a rood or reredos. Not all of them, perhaps, are of great aesthetic worth, but few have no capacity at all to allow the viewer to let the imagination off its leash and to lift up the heart to God.

During the time of my first incumbency, I came into contact with a movement which strongly influenced the subsequent course of my life because it gave me a number of very valuable insights about myself, about my own personal psychology. 'Clinical Theology', as it is called, explores the overlap between theology and psychiatry, not seeking to turn clergy into amateur psychiatrists (nor doctors into amateur theologians) but by enabling one to know oneself better, in order better to understand and help other people, especially through the skilled use of listening and pastoral counselling. The founder of the movement, Dr Frank Lake, sets out the underlying presupposition:

> This whole discipline of Clinical Theology depends on the truth of the Christian claim that in fellowship with God, through Christ and His Church, there are available personal resources which transform relationships and personality.[6]

Whilst Clinical Theology acknowledges its debt to Freud, Jung and Adler, it refuses to base its approach to the understanding of the human personality, in all its dimensions, on any one of them because, by implication, the 'norms' which they propose are mutually contradictory. Instead, it takes the life of Christ as the norm for its dynamic studies.

Part of my own debt to Clinical Theology is that it led to a deepening of my spirituality, since it was at this time that I discovered the works of the English mystics of the 14th-century, Richard Rolle, Julian of Norwich and Walter Hilton, *inter alia*. But it was the anonymous author of *The Cloud of Unknowing* who spoke to me most insistently about how God can be known. Part of the book's appeal to me is that it advocates no complicated intellectual system: mainly, though, it is because the author talks about a knowledge of God which comes to us through love.

To use spatial language, it is as if we lived in a five-decker universe: we are in the middle layer and separating us from the world, which is at the very bottom, is the Cloud of Forgetting. Above us, and separating us from God, who is at the very top, is the Cloud of Unknowing, which can be penetrated only by love. This can be shown in diagrammatic form:

God

The Cloud of Unknowing

Ourselves

The Cloud of Forgetting

The World

This concept has since become firmly established as part of my own understanding of Christian spirituality and has helped me to become increasingly aware of the many-sidedness of God. He is, as the theologians put it, 'transcendent', above all, greater than all; yet he is at the same time 'immanent', among us, involved with us. Further, he is at one and the same time our Creator, yet one with whom we can have a personal relationship, despite the fact that he is eternal and beyond time, whilst we are mortal and, in this life, within time.

As the first disciples of Jesus did, so we too can become aware that in some mysterious way he lives within us. As we each tread a different part of the pilgrims' way, we have to go at our own speed and not feel depressed because others seem to be so far ahead of us and getting to know God that much more quickly.

Chaucer's group – the Pardoner, the Miller, the Franklin, the Summoner, and all the rest of them – all trod the same path but each was at a different stage of spiritual development from the others, and that is how it has always been.

This chapter has been deliberately autobiographical in order to illustrate the course of one person's journey. The challenge which we all share is to go onwards in faith. One of the prime scriptural examples of one who travelled in faith is Jacob, the grandson of Abraham. In a passage which has been a constant source of encouragement to me, Jacob has a dream at Bethel in which God promises a great future for him and for his descendants. The passage is worth giving in full and amply repays careful thought:

> Jacob left Beer-sheba and went toward Haran. And he came to a certain place, and stayed there that night, because the sun had set. Taking one of the stones of the place, he put it under his head and lay down in that place to sleep. And he dreamed that there was a ladder set up on the earth, and the top of it reached to heaven; and behold, the angels of God were ascending and descending on it! And behold, the Lord stood above it and said, "I am the Lord, the God of Abraham your father and the God of Isaac; the land on which you lie I will give to you and to your descendants; and your descendants shall be like the dust of the earth, and you shall preach abroad to the west and to the east and to the north and to the south; and by you and your descendants shall all the families of the earth bless themselves. Behold, I am with you and will keep you wherever you go and will bring you back to this land; for I will not leave you until I have done that of which I have spoken to you.' Then Jacob awoke from his sleep and said, "Surely the Lord is in this place; and I did not know it." And he was afraid, and said, "How awesome is this place! This is none other than the house of God, and this is the gate of heaven." (Genesis 28.10–17)

The existence of God was evidently no problem for Jacob and I doubt if he found it necessary to justify his faith by intellectual processes. People living in the late twentieth-century appear to find God much more of a problem and we cannot simply urge upon them the need for faith. Alongside it must go a rational discussion of what we understand by God and in what sense we believe him to have an objective existence beyond our own minds.

If God is real and exists, the unambiguous logic and language of statements about existence, and the verification needed for these statements, must apply to God as much as to anything else, for these are part and parcel of what we mean by words like "exist" and "real"; but this is not to deny that much of His nature may be mysterious and uncomprehended by men.[7]

If God is real, then, is it possible to treat him as 'personal' in any meaningful sense of that word?

4 *Personality*

Because God is himself a 'person', he is one with whom we are able to have a personal relationship. Now the words *person* and *personality*, when they are used as technical theological descriptions of the attributes of God, no longer convey the same shade of meaning as they did when they were originally coined. Here once more we come up against the barrier of language: how **do** you find words which can adequately describe something which is beyond description, ineffable? And even if you think you have found such a word in *hypostasis*, the Greek word for substance, how do you translate it into intelligible English?

Our own finite personality severely restricts our ability even to conceive of God, let alone describe him. Yet the Bible, in both Old and New Testaments, portrays God as being personal, sometimes to the extent of anthropomorphism, as when Adam and Eve 'heard the sound of the Lord God walking in the garden in the cool of the day'. (Genesis 3.8)

The use of the word 'personality' in describing the attributes of God is bound to be an anthropomorphism, because it is a word specifically about humans and their relationships. 'Personhood', though an abstract word and therefore much less misleading, fails to convey much of what we commonly understand by 'personality', namely the outward expression of character, or that which makes evident a person's individuality, without which it would remain hidden, as if behind a mask.

If for the moment we think of the word 'God' as a symbol, something which stands for the highest good that we can possibly imagine, we then have to try to envisage what to us would be good *beyond* all imagining. I once had a heated and vigorous discussion with a fellow cleric about the priority of theology and psychology. He argued strongly that we must always start with theology, because you get nowhere until you bring God into the equation. I argued with equal vehemence that you have to make psychology the starting point, because you cannot begin to talk about God until you have begun to understand yourself. I suppose we were both right, and maybe I was influ-

enced too much by those lines of Alexander Pope in Epistle II of
An Essay on Man:

> Know then thyself, presume not God to scan;
> The proper study of mankind is man.

A possible synthesis is provided for us by the authors of an
article on God in *A New Dictionary of Christian Theology*:

> Knowledge of God is more and more recognized as being much
> more like personal knowledge than neutral, abstract or theoretical
> knowledge. In other words the appropriate response to him and the
> appropriate attitudes involved in such response are much more
> likely to emerge when he is conceived in personal rather than
> impersonal terms.[1]

If we are to believe Freud, many of whose insights into the
working of the human mind are truly invaluable, what we have
done with God is to create him in our own image by projecting
on to him our own particular idea of fatherhood.

> In more general terms, man, finding himself face to face with a
> potentially hostile world in which he knows all sorts of misfortunes
> and evils may happen to him, consoles and fortifies himself with
> belief in a benevolent God, who will probably shield him from
> disaster in this world, and certainly reward him with bliss hereafter.
> This Freud calls "wishful thinking".[2]

If Freud is wrong, as I believe he is in this matter, and if we are
made in God's image and not *vice versa*, then I can see nothing
improbable in that we should be able to know him. Indeed, the
more we can think of God in what we have called personal terms,
the more likely we are to move out of the rather sterile realm of
theory and into the living world of knowledge and relationships.
God then ceases to be a product of our own fantasies and dreams.

In conversation with a French philosopher, who happened to
be a Benedictine monk, the word 'experience' came up again and
again as we talked generally about epistemology and particularly
about the question of knowing God. He rightly insisted that we
would be most unwise to write this off as irrelevant: our own
experience **is** relevant to our knowledge of God, whether that

experience is of life as a whole or whether it is in that area which is primarily 'religious'. If we start with our ability to understand another person's situation, to enter into it as fully as we can, to experience it as though we were standing in his or her shoes, we can see the similarity between this familiar image on the one hand and the attempt to enter into a personal relationship with God on the other. We cannot, of course, stand where God is, but we can use our minds and our experience to place ourselves closer to him in thought and prayer. The experience will not leave us unchanged, and indeed may make us feel uncomfortable, because we have moved on from where we were, perhaps so imperceptibly that it is recognisable only when the experience has been repeated over and over again. Just as parts of our coastline are being eroded at a rate which can only be quantified in terms of centimetres per century, so it often is with our progress in the spiritual life: once in a while there may be a major upheaval which gains us more ground in an instant than we have achieved in a decade, but the forward movement is usually too gradual to be measured.

A similar process can take place when we spend any length of time listening to a piece of music, looking at a picture, or sitting in a cathedral and letting it speak to us: slowly we find that our minds have been enticed away from the music itself, or the painting, or the architecture, and our thoughts have developed more along the lines of worship. I do not mean that we are treating the object of our contemplation as an idol, rather that we have moved into the area of wonder, perhaps even of awe.

This process can also be formalised by the use of various devices to take up the automatic thinking part of our brain. The rosary is a good example within the Catholic tradition (both Roman and Anglican) and the Jesus Prayer in the Eastern Orthodox Church. Some oriental religious traditions make use of mandalas (symbolic paintings) and mantras (words) and these have gained a considerable respectability among Christians in recent decades. Two of the many contemporary western artists who have worked in this field are the American painter, Mark Rothko (1903–1970) whose great concern was that his paintings should be displayed in such a way as to create a mood of contemplation, and Craigie Aitchison (b.1926), who has spent much of his life painting very strange, yet profound, depictions of the crucifixion.

39

We can sometimes accelerate the process of moving into a deeper knowledge of God by tuning our imagination on to the wavelength of **myth**, not something which we all know to be untrue and little more than a fairy-tale but a way of representing the truth symbolically by means of a story. A good example of this is to be found in the description of creation at the start of Genesis: though not an accurate piece of historical or scientific writing, it nevertheless enshrines the fundamental truth that God is the Creator and that we are 'the people of his pasture, and the sheep of his hand'. (Psalm 95.7)

Our ability to know God would be very much greater if we had some way of forcing him to come out into the open, but would he then be the same God as he is now? No, because a god whom we can manipulate according to our own requirements is a creature of our own devising. Ultimately, it is an act of faith – both ours, and the realisation of his in us – which enables us to know anything at all about God, despite the arguments of those who assert that the Bible lays it all out before us and all the knowledge we need is to be found within its pages. Certainly we need the revelation which comes to us through scripture, for this is one of the primary witnesses of faith. We can recognise that through the agency of human beings, God has chosen to open our eyes to himself in the Old Testament, through the long tale of its history, the accumulated wisdom of centuries and the voice of prophecy. The process is continued more fully in the New Testament through the revelation of Christ in the Gospels, the Acts of the Apostles, the Epistles and the Apocalypse. But none of the historical events to which these works bear witness can compel us to believe in him. Professor James Mackey tells us that history can establish fairly certainly some facts about Jesus but that you cannot derive faith from them:

> Faith, with its own complement of quite specific convictions, can be offered as an interpretation of these historical facts; it can be laid alongside them so that correlations of claim or image can be noted … But … faith cannot be derived from them.[3]

It is the imagination, he adds, which 'gives access to the life of Jesus in his time and in ours'.

★　★　★

We turn now to three areas in which our personality seeks to unite itself with the personality of God, worship, literature and the arts. It is the experience of a wide diversity of Christian cultures, spread over nearly two millenia, and undergirded by a further two millenia of Jewish history, that worship (both private and corporate) is the primary mode of communion with God. What the wandering nomadic Hebrew tribes did, what was done by the Jews in home and temple and synagogue, what the early Christians did and others have done since, is the lifting up of the individual and of the community to the Creator. It is this which lies at the heart of all true knowledge of God, for faith cannot be separated from practice. The seed of worship is often sown when the human personality is at its very earliest stages of development. The plant into which it grows is an exceedingly tender one, needing careful cultivation over a long period of time. Yet it is this which is more likely to lead the soul to God than any amount of hard thinking, though this is not to deny the need for the exercise of cerebral activity as part of our pursuit of truth, goodness and beauty, all of which find their full fruition and fulfilment in God.

When we pray, we can actually allow our personality to speak up for itself, which is something we may not generally allow it to do in the normal conversations and happenings of daily life. If the prayer is to be truly expressive of ourselves, it will need to be totally honest, acknowledging all the bad things as well as being thankful for the good, offering all those negativities as being truly part of ourselves, the 'truth in the inward being' (Psalm 51.6): fear, hatred, anger, lust, greed, loneliness, dread, and all the rest of them. Because the best prayer is always two–directional, and the person who prays truly will be a listener as well as a speaker, we should also be prepared for some frank speaking from God.

It is possible to increase our understanding of God and our own self-understanding by making some passage of scripture personal to ourselves. You can, for example, turn St Paul's 'Hymn of Love' into a devotional exercise. To do so, you first read the text as it stands:

> Love is patient and kind; love is not jealous or boastful; it is not arrogant or rude. Love does not insist on its own way; it is not irritable or resentful; it does not rejoice at wrong, but rejoices in the right. Love bears all things, believes all things, hopes all things, endures all things. (1 Corinthians 13. 4–7)

41

Next, to see it from the Godward angle, you re-read it, this time changing the words 'love' and 'it', wherever they appear to 'Christ'. Then, to 'customize' it, you read the passage once more and replace those words with your own name.

A generation brought up on the Book of Common Prayer has been conditioned to believe, and rightly so, that we come to God as sinners in need of mercy and forgiveness, for such we are indeed. But this is not the same as lying down on the carpet and waiting to be kicked by God, or hoping that we can talk him out of whatever punishment he has in store for us. Nor, on the other hand, do we appear before God as an equal: the old proverb that 'man proposes but God disposes' is quite correct. Yet what we propose to God, and the way we set about it, is going to be strongly influenced by our own belief about the nature of the one to whom we pray. If we do actually believe him to be like the worst sort of traditional oriental (or occidental) despot, we will almost certainly be abasing ourselves vigorously, whereas if we believe him to be all that the best possible loving human parent, whether mother or father, could be, and then infinitely more besides, we shall approach him as one in whose love we can feel secure and confident. Most of us are somewhere in-between these two extremes and our prayers will reflect this accordingly.

In any scheme of private prayer there needs to be a proper balance between the essential ingredients, so that praise and thanksgiving find their rightful place alongside confession and intercession. As our prayer moves into the area of contemplation and meditation, we will probably develop more acutely the faculty of being still before God and of listening for his voice, so that the spiritual insight which he gives us helps us to see our own small-ness without undermining our essential personal integrity.

When it comes to public worship we have to be careful that we do not look on it as some kind of show put on for our own personal benefit, which we then judge according to the entertain-ment value we get out of it: 5 out of 10 for the music, 3 for the sermon, 8 for the readings. I suspect that the majority of regular churchgoers are subconsciously switched on and off by different aspects of the worship which they experience, in so far as these react in a positive or negative way with certain aspects of their personality, as well as being triggered off by their mood at the time. This makes it important that we should go to church with the expectation that we shall meet God there in our worship, even if not all parts of the service resonate with us to the same degree. In this way, we are less likely to come away disappointed by what we have experienced.

It is a fact of life, though, that the way in which the liturgy is done can deeply influence our own response to it. We all know about those services which have sent us on our way feeling depressed as well as those from which we have gone home with a real sense of having been with God. Occasional worshippers are at a great disadvantage here because we can only get the best out of the liturgy when we experience it in all its moods and in all ours as well. To be in church on Christmas Day is very wonderful and exciting, but even more so if we have just experienced an Advent with which to contrast it: similarly – and even more so – with Easter in relation to Lent and Holy Week.

One mark of a well-developed personality is its openness to the reception of new ideas, a lack of defensiveness when it comes to the possibility of change. It is interesting how quickly many congregations of all denominations have accepted the various changes of worship, both in structure and language, and it would be an instructive exercise to discover if there were any correlation between those who have welcomed change with reasonably good grace and the way in which that change has been introduced. I suspect that where a grudging and brief experiment has been made, and quickly abandoned, it is as a direct result of the lack of enthusiasm for change on the part of those responsible for initiating it.

It seems that we all have some areas in our life which we want to keep 'as it was in the beginning' and that might apply to such diverse matters as the food we eat, the daily paper we read, the version of the Bible we use in private, or the style of clothes we wear. Worship is an area in which we seem to be particularly conservative at first, but one where we are willing to move on when the reasons for doing so are clearly explained. Not surprisingly, when you have used a particular form of service all your life, you are not likely to take kindly to change all at once: it takes time to adjust and then we seem to settle down well until the next change is threatened ten or twenty years later, but at least by then we have got used to the idea that the liturgy is not something which is set in concrete.

43

If there is one strong justification for change, apart from purely liturgical factors, it is that changes make us think what we are doing when we worship. There needs to be a degree of subconscious activity within our personality when we are attending a church service, though this does not mean that we simply switch on the auto-pilot and do it all without thought, for when we lose sight of the purpose of worship, we lost sight of God.

In his *Reflections on the Psalms*, C. S. Lewis (1898–1963), one of the most influential of all the English Christian apologists of this century, writes about the differences between Jew and Greek: the former centred the delight of his religion on the Temple and all that it stood for: the latter, he says, was more analytical and logical. Then he goes on to draw a modern parallel:

> The sort of distinction which we can easily make between those who are really worshipping God in church and those who enjoy 'a beautiful service' for musical, antiquarian, or merely sentimental reasons, would have been impossible to them. We get nearest to their state of mind if we think of a pious modern farm-labourer at church on Christmas Day or at the harvest thanksgiving. I mean, of course, one who really believes, who is a regular communicant; not one who goes only on these occasions and is thus (not in the worst but in the best sense of that word) a Pagan, practising Pagan piety, making his bow to the Unknown and at other times Forgotten – on the great annual festivals. The man I picture is a real Christian. But you would do him wrong by asking him to separate out, at such moments, some exclusively religious element in his mind from all the rest – from his hearty social pleasure in a corporate act, his enjoyment of the hymns (and the crowd), his memory of other such services since childhood, his well-earned anticipation of rest after harvest or Christmas dinner after church. They are all one in his mind. This would have been truer of any ancient man, and especially of an ancient Jew. He was a peasant, very close to the soil. He had never heard of music, or festivity, or agriculture as things separate from religion, nor of religion as something separate from them. Life was one. This assuredly laid him open to spiritual dangers which more sophisticated people can avoid; it also gave him privileges which they lack.[4]

Lewis was, by profession, a teacher, a Professor of Medieval and Renaissance English. Reading A. N. Wilson's biography of Lewis leads me to ask what it must have been like to have been taught by this multi-faceted person, with his curious relationships in private life, his enormous command of the subject he taught and his deep commitment to Christianity. He is one of those rare authors with the gift of linking theology and literature without doing injustice to either and without loss of integrity. To both he brought a creative imagination and, in his own novels, whether they were intended primarily for adults or primarily for young people, there is never the feeling that he is hard at work punching home a message. As with his contemporary, J. R. R. Tolkien (1892–1973), Lewis allows the reader to enter into the experience of the characters he creates and to let their personalities speak to that of the reader. And yet the religious message is there all the time for those who are both able and willing to perceive it.

There seems to be a stage in literature where neither skill nor imagination alone is responsible for what is produced; at some point there comes an additional factor which lifts the writer into a realm where the 'spiritual' takes over, whether or not this occurs in the context of a life consciously lived in the power of God. This is true of any great creative activity and appears with a particularly luminous quality in music. Bach's *B minor Mass* and *St Matthew Passion* are works of consummate skill but they are much more than this, as if the personality of the composer has been either invaded or transcended in some mysterious way to enable him to bring us a message which comes from God. When I remember how the Principal of my Theological College used to define the priest as one who stood on the Godward side of man and on the manward side of God, I find myself thinking that the same is true of those who are messengers of the divine Spirit in the artistic world, too.

When we listen to music, when we look at a painting, a piece of sculpture or a building, when we read a poem or a novel, when we watch a play or a ballet, although we may have nothing else in our minds than to pass an hour or two enjoyably, the effect which that activity has on us is not limited to some particular part of us labelled 'entertainment' or 'aesthetic experience'. It is total. 'It affects us as entire human beings; it affects our moral and religious existence', writes T. S. Eliot in an article entitled 'Religion and Literature'.[5]

The whole of that complex entity which we call our personality becomes involved in these activities: our bodies (especially our physical senses), our minds, our souls. The complex psychosomatic system is at work and no part of us remains untouched by the experience, however unaware we may be that this is so.

Few writers have brought this home to me more vividly than David Jones. His works need time spent on them to grasp what they are all about, but the imagery in them is extraordinarily powerful. *In Parenthesis*, published in 1936, looks back to the First World War and recalls the memories of the life of a soldier in those awful trenches. Here are a few characteristic lines:

> The terrain of bivouac was dark wrapt; the moon was in her most diminished quarter.

> It was useless trying to sleep with all this trapesing about – and the more clumsy ones tripping over the pegged-down ground-sheet, or poking in-under, to ask if you were "A" Company – or Sergeant Coke of "C" – or Mr Talbot's batman.

> Besides which there was the heavy battery operating just beneath the ridge, at a kept interval of minutes, with unnerving inevitability, as a malign chronometer, ticking off with each discharge an exactly measured progress towards a certain and prearranged hour of apocalypse.

> Private Saunders lay, one of three, under the low-sagged vaulting or laced-together bivvy sheets, like a hare's form, that they had there constructed on the open down.

> The whole valley was dotted in roughly ordered lines with such improvised shelters as men could devise; and here and there a tent half-heartedly camouflaged, where a commander sought his sleep – or cursed by candlelight ambiguous countermanding chits. These three of them sucked Mackintosh's toffee where they lay, and littered the narrow burrow with tiny grease-proof paper twists. The post-corporal had tossed him the parcel when he went down to the water-cart.

> The 9-inch kept its interval of fire. Then a companion battery opened out with its full complement – and yet lesser pieces further forward, over the ridge, spread up fans of light and from the deeper part of the valley, where by day there seemed nothing other than a stretched tarpaulin and branches artfully spread, eight bright tongues licked, swift as adder-fangs darted. The candle-end by the toffee-tin, flickered and went out – they let it be, and watched the relaying flashes play again.[6]

Sixteen years later came the *The Anathemata*, which tells the story of our land and its people from the days long before the coming of humanity. A complex variety of themes interweaves thoughts from the Roman Catholic Mass, Malory's *Morte D'Arthur*, popular songs, classical mythology, the Welsh language, children's rhymes, Scripture and many other sources.

Canon Allchin has written an article in *Theology* called 'A Discovery of David Jones' and in it he analyses the major structural content of the poet's work:

> David Jones, both in writing and in the visual arts, is concerned throughout with the vision of this world as God's world. Two of the central themes in his activity are sacrament and anamnesis. Heaven and earth are full of God's glory. But it is really this earth in which the glory is to be revealed, not some fantasy world, nor some select and insulated corner of the whole of reality.[7]

It is one of the aspirations of the artist to reflect what he sees of this world and to interpret it, to mediate it to the rest of us so that we can see it, if not through his own eyes, then at least from a different viewpoint from our own. An artist friend of mine has told me how he had seen on a visit to the National Gallery a crucifix which made him go weak at the knees, so much so that he took with him on a subsequent visit someone whom he knew to be contemplating suicide and the painting had a similarly beneficial effect on him, too. For these two people, that particular work at that particular time had been a very real experience, though one should not assume that the same effect would be produced on every other person who saw it. It would be as unreasonable to conclude that every painting should hold the same message for every viewer as to suppose that every piece of music will speak in the same way to everyone who hears it or that every poem will illuminate the understanding of everyone who reads it to precisely the same degree. Each time it happens, we can only receive the experience after it has been filtered through our own personality and, as it occurs, it will change that personality, perhaps imperceptibly, but sometimes dramatically.

The story is told of Count von Zinzendorff who, having time to kill in a provincial German town, drifted into a museum and found himself in front of a painting of the crucifixion beneath which were written the words, 'All this I did for you: what have you done for me?' He was still there hours later when the caretaker came to lock up, but the experience entered so deeply into his personality that his whole life changed from that moment and he went on to become the founder and pastor of the 'Herrnhut' community.

What are the criteria for judging a work of art? Clearly one of them has to be the effect it has on the viewer, which of course is largely a subjective matter. For example, when we are sizing up an architectural work, we are literally doing just that, among other things: we are sizing it up, noting its dimensions, as well as the general shape, design, colour, lighting and materials. The other principal criterion is the intrinsic quality of the work itself, the way it has been conceived and executed, which depends very considerably on the personality of the architect. What is his own experience of life, how was he trained, what is his ability in the technical sense, how good is he at his job, what degree of creativity does he bring to it, how lively is his imagination? It is a very natural response to a work of art to consider oneself as its judge: sometimes, though, we should turn that process on its head and remember that **it** is also judging **us**. Because the finished work is not the only factor in the creation of a work of art, we should give due thought to the process by which it came about: this, at least for the creator, is probably as important as what has been produced, and it is one of the elements through which the judgement is made on ourselves.

We may be aware of a tendency within ourselves to write off as worthless anything that gives us no personal aesthetic satisfaction. This is a disease which has a habit of intensifying as we grow older and as we become more set in our ways, knowing what we like and above all liking what we know. By doing this, we are denying the possibility of change and progress, either in the world of art or in our own aesthetic experience, and this is bound to result in an impoverishment of our personality. It is as if an English person were to say that no good music has been written since Elgar and Vaughan Williams, no good painting done since Constable and Turner and no good buildings put up since Wren and Nash.

Each of us, including the artist, is involved in the on-going creative act of God, every second of every day. To do so fully, we have to remain open and vulnerable, knowing that this may cause us the pain of losing our apparent securities.

We may well be right in our assumption that some modern art is bad, either in itself or (as is also the case in architecture) in relation to its surroundings. But because modernity does not appeal to us, we are on very dangerous ground if we declare it to be useless. Much of the artistic work of the 20th-century has been responsible for opening the eyes of two or three successive generations to a new perspective of what is beautiful, even if (or perhaps because) it is seeking to interpret afresh the realities of everyday life. The paintings of Francis Bacon, who often stated that his pictures are not intended to convey a specific meaning but are 'an attempt to make a certain type of feeling visual'; the music of Arnold Schönberg which, with its conspicuous atonality, broke many of the established harmonic conventions; the architecture of Richard Rogers, with its pioneering technology, as seen in the Pompidou Centre in Paris and the Lloyds building in the city of London; and the poems of Roger McGough, such as *My cat and i*, which iconoclastically has the lower case *i* in each of its three verses and eschews all punctuation marks: these are not to everybody's taste, but it is hard to deny their creative vitality.

Artists, whether ancient or modern, can only go so far in taking us along the avenue of aesthetics. They can point us, lead us, even cajole us: but the final say has to be ours and ours alone. Only we can hope to find the personal answers to the really big problems with which our personalities have to engage, the ultimate questions as to the meaning of life, our own part in it, and our relationship to God. It is one of the glories of our humanity that things of beauty can create for us a sort of timelessness in which everything seems to be just right.

The experience, when it comes, is all too rare and all too brief but I believe it to be an experience through which we can know the transcendent God. In knowing him like this, we also know the meaning of St Paul's words about 'the fruit of the Spirit': among the ones he lists in Galatians 5.22–23, the first three, love, joy and peace, seem to be very much the ones which come to us in those moments *when words fail*. But knowledge is not the same thing as commitment: in the end there has to be an act of faith, through which our own personality enters into a deeper relationship with God, its Creator.

5 *Power*

'It all depends on what you mean by ...'. These words were frequently on the lips of that eminent broadcaster, Dr C. E. M. Joad, who became extremely well-known to a generation which listened to a radio programme called the *Brains Trust*, in which questions were put to a panel of entertaining and erudite speakers, a prototype of the later *Any Questions?* and television's *Question Time*. Dr Joad was a stickler for identifying precisely what was being discussed: anything remotely woolly was seized on and shaken until it yielded its proper meaning. It is a catchphrase still in use today and not infrequently heard in a court of law, where judge and jury are attempting to ascertain the truth. Philosophers (and Joad was one himself) use the phrase every day as they seek to identify just what is meant by a particular statement, so that there can be no doubt or misunderstanding about it.

We have to do the same thing when we talk about God: it all depends on what we mean by God. **You** know what **you** mean by God but it may not be the same as **I** mean. Unfortunately, there is no easy definition with which everyone can agree, as there is if we are discussing some everyday object such as a vacuum cleaner, an orange, or a railway train. There is no argument about them because they are things which we come across regularly and can define without overmuch difficulty. God is different: he is *sui generis*. Even though we have a wide vocabulary of words which are frequently used to describe him, adjectives such as Almighty, Everlasting and Eternal, and nouns such as Creator, Father and King, these words cannot have precisely the same meanings as we normally attach to them because human vocabulary is incapable of providing words to describe what is totally outside our human knowledge and experience.

So in this chapter, the title of which is one of those three attributes ascribed to God in the longer ending of the Lord's Prayer, we examine our understanding of God in relation to aesthetics.

Almost the final words of one of the three New Testament letters attributed to Saint John comprises this statement:

> We know that the Son of God has come and has given us under-
> standing, to know him who is true; and we are in him who is true,
> in his Son Jesus Christ. (1 John 5.20)

This knowledge which we have through Jesus Christ is very much more than the summation or the culmination of that knowledge of God which had already been revealed to the Jews in their scriptures, the Old Testament. The knowledge of God about which John speaks is the final and complete revelation of God, manifested in this world of space and time, as his incarnate Son, Jesus Christ, and made known through what he was, what he said and what he did, particularly in his death and resurrection.

We can legitimately ask just how God revealed himself before the coming of Christ. The Old Testament points us in a number of directions: God's original creative act in Genesis; the history of his people, Abraham and his descendants; the mighty act of deliverance recorded in Exodus, through which the people of God were led to the Promised Land under Moses; the Covenant, which God entered into with them; the further act of deliverance by which the people of God were freed from their Exile in Babylon; together with all the other events of their salvation history, as well as through the voices of prophets and sages, priests and kings.

That Covenant laid certain obligations on the Jewish people: in order to know God in all these various ways, they were to obey God, trust God and love God. God is already a fact of life: nowhere is there any question about his existence and nowhere do the Old Testament writers make any real effort to argue for it.

By such means, the Jewish people were prepared for the final revelation of God in the coming of Jesus as the child of Bethlehem, the man of sorrows and the victor over death. They were able to co-operate with God as he made himself known in what one New Testament writer describes as 'many and various ways' (Hebrews 1.1), but the first move came from God himself: it is he who opens the channels of communication.

Our response to God in prayer demonstrates that there is that within us which turns us towards him in the first place. To use a spatial metaphor, somewhere in the innermost depths of our being there is an innate tendency towards God which enables us consciously to become aware of our relationship with him. Even the very word 'God' has to be invented by man to give a name to the one who has no name. It adds nothing to our knowledge of God yet it is the last utterance that we can make on our side of the line beyond which words fail. This is what is being asserted here by Karl Rahner:

> The concept "God" is not a grasp of God by which a person masters the mystery, but it is letting oneself be grasped by the mystery which is present yet ever distant. This mystery remains a mystery even though it reveals itself to man.[1]

There is a well-known painting by William Holman Hunt (1827–1910) dating from 1853, of which the original is in Keble College, Oxford, and a replica in St Paul's Cathedral. It portrays Jesus with a lamp in his hand, standing outside a closed door. The viewer observes that there is no handle on the outside of the door, an impression which is reinforced by the title of the painting, 'Behold, I stand at the door and knock' (Revelation 3.20). Only from within the human soul can the response be made to the call of God. Outside (and yet all the while within) God is there, not preparing to break down the door, but patiently waiting.

This is an interesting reversal of what Jesus says in the Gospels: there, he instructs **us** to be the ones who knock:

> Ask, and it will be given you; seek, and you will find; knock, and it will be opened to you. (St Matthew 7.7)

There, too, it is he himself who is the door (St John 10.7). Now all this is turned round, so that it is **he** who knocks at **our** door. In his *Commentary on the Epistles to the Seven Churches in Asia*, Archbishop Trench pointed out that Jesus not only knocks: he speaks as well, and thus there can be no doubt as to who it is who is out there seeking entry.

The origins of this image are almost certainly to be found in the Old Testament book, 'The Song of Solomon', or 'Canticles', as it is sometimes called, a series of sensuous oriental love poems in which the same picture appears:

> I slept, but my heart was awake. Hark! my beloved is knocking. 'Open to me, my sister, my love, my dove, my perfect one; for my head is wet with dew, my locks with the drops of the night.' I had put off my garment, how could I put it on? I had bathed my feet,

how could I soil them? My beloved put his hand to the latch, and my heart was thrilled within me. I arose to open to my beloved, and my hands dripped with myrrh, my fingers with liquid myrrh, upon the handles of the bolt. I opened to my beloved, but my beloved had turned and gone. My soul failed me when he spoke. I sought him, but found him not; I called him, but he gave no answer. (Song of Solomon 5.2–6)

The author of 'Revelation' leaves it to the reader as to whether or not the call of Christ is answered.

God is described by one Old Testament writer in terms which to a generation brought up on alleged sightings of Unidentified Flying Objects suggests the arrival of some kind of spaceship, with its turning wheels and 'something like burning coals of fire, like torches moving to and fro' (Ezekiel 1.13). The writer himself was in no doubt that he had seen something of God: not, you will notice, 'the Lord'; nor 'the glory of the Lord'; nor even 'the likeness of the glory of the Lord'; but 'the appearance of the likeness of the glory of the Lord' (Ezekiel 1.28). Those theologians and mystics who have come closest to this radiating power have become aware of the utter beauty of the Lord: they may not have come to this awareness by intellectual processes but they have 'seen' and 'known' God.

We who live on a less exalted plane are more likely to come to this kind of awareness of the glory and beauty of the Lord either through our personal devotions, including our meditating on the life of Jesus, or through our corporate worship, particularly the Eucharist, where the presence of Christ is given physical expression in the sacramental bread and wine, as we respond to his command, 'Do this in remembrance of me'. (St Luke 22.19; 1 Corinthians 11.24–25)

By the time we reach this point in the service of Holy Communion, we have already expressed in the Creed our belief in 'one God, the Father, the almighty, maker of heaven and earth, of all that is, seen and unseen'. Then, at the moment of communion, we take into our innermost being the power which one scriptural author describes as:

that which was from the beginning, which we have heard, which we have seen with our eyes, which we have looked upon and touched with our hands. (1 John 1.1)

That is not the time to argue for or against the existence of God: it is the time to 'behold the fair beauty of the Lord' and to glory in the promise made to Thomas:

> Blessed are those who have not seen and yet believe. (St John 20.29)

Anyone who is a regular attender at church services of any denomination will realise that what goes on in them cannot be separated from what we believe, because our worship gives expression to our belief. That is one reason why it is customary to recite one of the traditional creeds at most of our services. It is not only at public services that we can both believe and worship, worshipping because we believe and believing because our worship leads us to do so. Every time we say the simplest of prayers we are placing ourselves in the presence of God, and it is always possible for us to experience something of his reality when we do so. This is the basis of all mysticism: a power beyond all human power impinges on, or even breaks through into, our awareness.

> God is, and lives, confessed by man or not. By his loving action among and with and upon us, focussed in worship, he takes us up into his own life.[2]

The only name which we have for this power or principle is the name 'God'. In his theological introduction to the Thirty-Nine Articles of the Church of England, Professor Bicknell defines God as:

> the one self-existent Being, the Author and Sustainer of all that is, upon whom all things depend and in whom they find their goal.[3]

A more authoritative view is to be found in the report published in 1938 of the Commission on Christian Doctrine. In answer to the question, 'What do we mean by the word God?', it comments as follows:

> It has been said that "God is the living Being who is at once the ultimate existence and the supreme and all-inclusive good"; and, again, that "God is that which we can, and must, worship." These two formulae may be taken as starting-points, the one as an initial statement of what God is in Himself, the other of what God is in relation to us.[4]

There is a fine poetic passage which, because it is in the Apocrypha, seldom finds its way into the minds of Christians:

> For all men who were ignorant of God were foolish by nature; and they were unable from the good things that are seen to know him who exists, nor did they recognize the craftsman while paying heed to his works; but they supposed that either fire or wind or swift air, or the circle of the stars, or turbulent water, or the luminaries of heaven were the gods that rule the world.
>
> If through delight in the beauty of these things men assumed them to be gods, let them know how much better than these is their Lord, for the author of beauty created them. And if men were amazed at their power and working, let them perceive from them how much more powerful is he who formed them. For from the greatness and beauty of created things comes a corresponding perception of their Creator.
>
> Yet these men are little to be blamed, for perhaps they go astray while seeking God and desiring to find him. For as they live among his works they keep searching, and they trust in what they see, because the things that are seen are beautiful. Yet again, not even they are to be excused; for if they had the power to know so much that they could investigate the world, how did they fail to find sooner the Lord of these things? (Wisdom 13.1–9)

The writer clearly believes that it is possible for us to know the power of God by opening our eyes and looking around us and seeing him in the things that are beautiful in this world. Even if we put up the shutters, not just of our eyes but of our hearts and minds too, that will not cause God to disappear.

*   *   *

Whatever else one might want to add to the various attempts at defining the indefinable, one would certainly want to stress that when we talk about God we are not discussing something abstract: God is neither some *thing* nor some abstraction: we are talking about some *one*, someone who is real, as real as electricity, as real as DNA, as real as the air we breathe. But no definition will ever be completely satisfactory, at least for the Christian, unless it emphasises that 'God' means God the Holy Trinity. It is only this understanding of God that can give us a more adequate concept of him than can be achieved by the mere word 'God'. It is possible for our reason to take us to the point of believing in the existence of God, but we can only know that he is Father, Son and Holy Spirit because this is how he has chosen to reveal himself to us.

Although the Bible itself knows nothing of a formal doctrine of the Trinity, it is nevertheless a belief which is drawn directly from scripture. It starts with the experience of those who knew Jesus Christ (either in the flesh or by reputation) and who also experienced the working and the power of the Holy Spirit; they believed that in each was to be found a manifestation of God.

For Jews, whose religious upbringing was strictly monotheistic, reflection on this mystery must have been immensely puzzling: how was it possible for the Creator to be God, for Jesus himself to be God, and for the Holy Spirit to be God, without there being three gods?

It took several centuries for the Church's understanding of the Trinity to be worked out fully, with its doctrine of three Persons in one God, the Father who creates us, the Son who redeems us and the Spirit who sanctifies us (God **over** us, God **with** us, and God **in** us).

* * *

These theological reflections must now be set in the context of aesthetics, first with architecture and sculpture, and using as our starting point the word 'numinous'. The *Oxford Dictionary of the Christian Church* tells us that this word was coined by the German theologian, Rudolf Otto (1869–1937) to denote the sense of awe and self-abasement which is brought about by the experience of 'holiness'. Presumably he would have used it to describe such experiences as those of Jacob at Bethel (Genesis 28.10–22) and of Moses at the Burning Bush (Exodus 3.1–6). The numinous is a term which we might well use to describe our experience of any holy place which gives us that sense of overpowering wonder. Whether or not we would wish nowadays to make such a sharp distinction between what is holy and what is not holy, between 'sacred' and 'secular', the concept of the numinous remains a valuable one. Had the word been invented a little earlier, it might well have spoken with great clarity to the eminent Victorian architect,

John Loughborough Pearson, whose avowed aim in designing the neo-Gothic 1880s cathedral at Truro was to build 'that which would bring men soonest to their knees'. This was an era when it was deemed almost mandatory for any new church to be built in that particular style, or any old one to be restored in it, as if there were a proper ecclesiastical style of architecture which alone could convey the sense of the holy. Indeed, even at the end of the twentieth-century, we have not fully escaped from that way of thinking.

Much as I warm to the totally different style of Liverpool's Roman Catholic Cathedral, there is still a part of me that enjoys from the aesthetic point of view the soaring arches and pinnacles, the distant vistas and open spaces of the real Gothic style, which speaks to me of the numinous in a way that a Renaissance, Baroque, Roccoco, Regency or Georgian building seldom does. For sheer purity of style and aesthetic appeal my preference is for the final flowering of the Romanesque, as seen for example in the south choir arcade of Romsey Abbey, dating from the years 1120 to 1140, which conveys to me a real sense of the power of God and the beauty of God, though I readily acknowledge that this is very much a matter of individual taste.

One cannot avoid large buildings, architecturally good or bad, because of their sheer size, and one is faced day in and day out with literature, music and painting. Our contact with sculpture, though, is much less frequent and usually has to be sought out rather than being stumbled upon by accident. For that reason we probably find it much harder to judge what our feelings about it are. If what we see is no more than a good workmanlike copy of the original form, it is hardly likely to stick in our minds as an exciting piece of sculpture, accurate though it may be as a representation of, say, the Madonna and Child.

Two carvings on the grand scale which have impressed me enormously are a couple of examples of that familiar French work of art, the Calvaire, the depiction (often by the roadside) of the Crucifixion of Jesus, with St Mary, St John and attendant angels. The ones at Plougastal Daouglas and Guimilau in Brittany are colossal, with around two hundred carved figures on each, executed in a strikingly primitive style with, for instance, a luxuriously bewhiskered and hatted St Joseph or a small band of wandering musicians accompanying the procession to Calvary.

When we go into an English church or cathedral close and see a piece of sculpture which bears a passing resemblance to an outsize piece of Emmenthal cheese, we may at first be taken aback. 'What on earth is it?' we ask, with perhaps a trace of cynicism or disbelief in our voice, but it is frequently this kind of unusual piece which will have more to say to us than the straightforward lines of something more obvious. In asking the question, we are beginning to explore the significance. Is it a Virgin and Child? Is it something entirely abstract? What does it say to me?

Now it may well be that we have come across what is essentially not merely an ugly sculpture but a bad one, one which signally fails to testify to the beauty and power of God, the creator of all things. Or it may be one that gives us a profound sense of aesthetic satisfaction, because it has the power to move us another step on our pilgrimage as seekers after beauty, truth and goodness. Much of the work of Elizabeth Frink, who died in 1993, has this effect on many who see it, a good example being her sculpture at Salisbury Cathedral of Mary, now no longer the young virgin mother but the mature woman, who has seen her son die on the cross and has helped to hold together the little band of followers.

★   ★   ★

Hans Küng, in his book *Art and the Question of Meaning*, maintains that it is the task of members of the artistic community to avoid merely copying the work of the past as if to say that God cannot be found in the present but only in some particular historical situation. Equally they are to avoid the other extreme of totally rejecting the past and centering entirely on the future. The paramount work of the artist, he says, is to tackle the ultimate questions.

> For the artist it should be of the utmost importance not to leave unanswered the great questions of ground and meaning ... Also ... it should be of the utmost importance to know *whence we come, whither we are going, who we are.*[5]

This sense of direction in the artist is complementary to the purpose of the art itself in drawing the viewer's thoughts to a point beyond himself or herself. Although specifically religious subjects have not been much on the painter's agenda since Victorian days, partly as a reaction to the sheer ghastliness of some of them, and partly as a reflection of the general decline of religion since then, the lamp has been kept burning by a succession of painters who have maintained some kind of spiritual vision, among them Van Gogh, Stanley Spencer and Marc Chagall.

★   ★   ★

Music has been much better served both by composers with deep personal commitment to the Christian faith and by choirs and individuals able and willing to perform their works. The continuing strength of cathedral music, with its widening repertoire embracing works of every age including the most up-to-date, together with the extraordinary skill and dedication of those who perform it, are very encouraging signs of artistic and religious strength. Music, when it forms part of the liturgy, has a power of its own to transform the words and the worshipper and to serve as a medium by which the things of this world encounter the things of the other world. Like the stable at Bethlehem, music can provide a cradle for the coming of Christ into the world of humanity.

One composer whose works exemplify this power to the most amazing degree is J. S. Bach (1685–1750). It has become clear that Bach was much more than a composer of unparalleled genius. He was also a deeply convinced Christian with a depth of spirituality which finds an immediately recognisable expression in his musical output: not for nothing did he have dozens of books on all aspects of the Christian faith in his own personal collection.

Perhaps the greatest literary equivalent of Bach is to be found in fourteenth-century Italy, in the person and works of the poet Dante (1265–1321), a man devoted to the church's ministry of word and sacrament, yet forced to spend a third of his life in a kind of peripatetic exile. His major work, the 'Divine Comedy' (*La Divina Commedia*) is not, as its title might suggest, a humorous work but is the story in three stages of the journey of the human soul through the life of the world to come, with its 'Inferno', 'Purgatorio' and 'Paradiso'.

Three guides are present to assist the soul towards the attainment of the Beatific Vision. The first is the Roman poet, Virgil, who stands in the poem as the representative of unsanctified human reason; then comes Beatrice, a mysterious figure with whom, or with whose memory, Dante was in love for much of his life, and who here stands for human reason which has seen the light of God's revelation; and finally there is St Bernard, the early twelfth-century scholar, monk and statesman, who now represents the mystical way to God and through whom Dante meets Mary the Mother of Jesus on his way to the vision of God in heaven. Here is a masterpiece of rare aesthetic quality, an outstanding work of genius, but a genius indubitably motivated and inspired by God.

Such a work as the 'Divine Comedy' actually operates on two distinct, if interrelated, levels. On the one hand it provides a profound insight into the spiritual dimensions of life and death (as does Newman's *Dream of Gerontius* to a lesser degree) and on the other hand it derives an equal share of its vitality and strength from its working on the plane of human experience, both that of the writer and that of the reader.

One of the literary giants of our own time, T. S. Eliot, was considerably influenced by Dante, among others. Born in Missouri, U.S.A., in 1888, he later became a British citizen and his poetry reflects the different stages of his spiritual journey, from the agnosticism of *Prufrock* (1917) to the faith of *Murder in the Cathedral* (1935) and the mysticism of *Four Quartets* (1935–1942). This series of meditations on time and timelessness ranks among the major works of spiritual writing of all ages and comes from within the poet's own specific experience of the world, of himself, and of God, and from his pondering on the great mysteries of creation and redemption, in which the power of God is seen in its most awe-inspiring light.

* * *

At the centre of everything is God: but this is not how we usually perceive it. Our human view tends to reverse reality by putting ourselves at the centre of everything, with other people revolving around us like satellites. Somewhere, vaguely 'out there', is God. An essential element of Christian spirituality is that we come to see ourselves in our rightful place in relation to God, the God of nature, science, theology and art, the God who has shown himself to be so much more than the power at the centre of the universe:

God is spirit, and those who worship him must worship him in spirit and in truth (St John 4.24).

One of the most astounding of all paradoxes is that the all-powerful God is he who, in Christ, stoops to wear our humanity. It is to this, and other paradoxes, that we now turn.

6 *Paradox*

Like so many of the words in the English language, the word 'paradox' comes to us from the Greek, in fact from two Greek words, one meaning 'against' or 'contrary to' and the other meaning 'opinion'. So when the two are put together, you have something that goes against received opinion, or something that seems contrary to what our common sense tells us, and yet is true. In its wider application, the word paradox is also used for any statement or action which is inherently self-contradictory, but which expresses a larger truth.

In Volume 3 of *Herrlichkeit*, his massive study of theological aesthetics, the Swiss theologian Hans Urs von Balthasar writes of Dante as:

> a personality to which nothing human, but also nothing divine, is alien, a personality that stretches out to the furthermost limits of the cosmos and pursues its own Christian fulfilment within the cosmic context of the fulfilment of the Kingdom of God. This leads directly to the central paradox that, as a created reality, this person will attain the heights of fame, but as a Christian reality, he will at the same time be thrust down into the profoundest humility and humiliation.[1]

Even when he is dealing with a concept as fundamental as the major Christian paradox of 'the first shall be last and the last first', and even when his work is translated into English, von Balthasar's writing is by no means easy going, yet no one has come up with a work on the theology of beauty to match *The Glory of the Lord*. His theme is that beauty can be perceived in every aspect of the theologian's field of study, with Jesus Christ at the heart of it as the truest of all manifestations of beauty, since he himself is God.

We are able to experience something of this beauty in the person of Jesus Christ and in this world which he has redeemed, but the full glory must await our ultimate vision of God. In Volume 4, 'The Realm of Metaphysics in Antiquity', the author quotes with approval the proverb of the ancient Greek philosopher, Plato, that 'the beautiful is difficult', because the word 'beautiful' in its original sense also included what was right and fitting and good, 'that in virtue of which it possesses its integrity, its health, its security'.

We see something of the truth of this in the artist's struggle to communicate beauty in a world where, for many, there is not even meaning, let alone beauty. The artist must bear some of the responsibility for this dilemma for, although he or she reflects the contemporary thinking of humanity, with all its doubts and uncertainties, the artist has from time to time rejected the traditional aesthetic values. Some of this refusal to conform can be attributed to the rejection by society as a whole of those profound spiritual insights which come only from within the Christian experience of faith: if that which gives ultimate meaning to life as a whole is missing, we need not be surprised to find that meaninglessness is a recurring theme in the world of the painter, the writer and the musician.

Since the mid-1950s I have enjoyed reading the novels of Iris Murdoch, though some of them have left me feeling somewhat uneasy: perhaps that is their intention. I do not know the reason but I suspect that it is something to do with a feeling that the world as she sees it **is** an odd place, full of odd people, with a somewhat peculiar, even morbid, slant to its highly introspective spiritual dimension, and yet it is a world which is very much alive and kicking. That I find paradoxical, even alarming.

A similar effect is produced when I hear certain modern music: my musical friends tell me that I need educating to it but my instinct (not, I admit, something always to be trusted implicitly) tells me that there is within it a dissonance which could be either a deliberate attempt to break with the norms of the past or yet another reflection of our being out of tune with the universe and with its creator. Maybe the explanation is the eminently simple one that I have spent a lifetime believing that an octave consists of twelve semitones, not nine or seventeen, and whatever conflicts with this built-in notion goes against my own personal musical grain. Whatever the reason may be, it leaves me with a sense of mental, spiritual and even sometimes physical disquiet. Without wishing to labour the point, we could probably all point to works of other kinds which produce the same depressing effect: a tasteless painting, a tortuous piece of sculpture, a building which sticks out like a very sore thumb on an otherwise wholesome hand.

From my conversations with writers, artists, musicians and

architects, and from my own observation of their work, I suspect that the harder they try to come up with something which is beautiful, the more unlikely they are to produce it. Paradoxically, it seems as if beauty is a kind of side-product of the creative process itself, not something to be striven for *per se*, rather as happiness in our lives seldom comes when it is deliberately pursued, but has a habit of making itself felt when we are not expecting it. As I hinted in Chapter 2, the search for truthfulness is in many ways more valid than the pursuit of beauty.

One of the tasks of the artist is to make manifest that which is hidden, to bring into the light of day something which would otherwise never see it. Let me explain this by an illustration. One of the more unconventional representations of the crucifixion of Jesus is Salvador Dali's *Christ of St John of the Cross*. It is a vision of the event as seen from an unconventional perspective, from above, with the crucified Lord bathed in light against a dark background, below which there are first clouds, then a layer of blue sky and then a lake with hills rising from its edge. In the foreground is a fishing boat with a figure standing beside it, whilst another person lays out the nets on the shore. That particular way of looking at that particular happening would probably not occur to many people, yet it has always been there as a possibility. In Dali's striking painting, the possibility becomes a reality, the secret is revealed, and our minds are opened to a fresh approach to something which may have become over-familiar in its more characteristic portrayals.

Stanley Spencer (1892–1959) achieves a similar effect in his work, bizarre and uncomfortable as it may seem to the casual eye. If there are three words which let us into the secret of that work, they are *Crookham*, the Thames-side locus of his early environment; *Scripture*, themes from which are a recurring feature of his painting; and *War*, in the heart of which he found himself as a young man. In *The Last Supper* (1920), his observation of the world around him provides little more in this picture than the very detailed red and brown bricks of the walls of the room in which the meal is being held. The remainder is pure imagination, with the robes and bare feet of the disciples stealing the scene even from Jesus, its central figure. Whatever else it does, it makes one look at the event in a new light and ponder its significance in a new way, which was presumably what the artist intended.

The distinction between the 'sacred' and the 'secular' is, as we have seen, in many respects an artificial one. What is secular today can become sacred tomorrow. When, in 1550, John Merbecke wrote the most famous of all the musical settings for the words of the Prayer Book service of Holy Communion, he drew on the popular melodies of the time, as J. S. Bach was to do 150 years later for some of his church music. In our own time, Eric Coates's *Dam Busters* march was used as the tune for the 'Sanctus' in a 1950s Folk Mass. A friend of mine reports that, on a recent visit to Mallorca, he attended Mass on the feast of Pentecost at the Roman Catholic Church in Pollensa, during which the Gloria was sung to the tune of 'John Brown's Body'!

One twentieth-century composer who has carved a particular niche for himself in this way is Ralph Vaughan Williams, who has neatly turned a number of English folk melodies into first-class hymn tunes: some good examples are *Kingsfold*, sung to 'I heard the voice of Jesus say', *Rodmell*, for 'When Christ was born in Bethlehem' and *Kings Lynn*, to 'The Church's one foundation'.

Vaughan Williams wrote much more than church music but, as with many other composers, one needs to weigh not the total volume of his more specifically Christian output but the quality of it as compared with the almost robotic output of anthems for all seasons of certain lesser musicians. One of the things that even the most accomplished composer can never achieve is to do what only the listener can do, which is to set what he hears within the context of his own world and of his own life. In this way the music helps to give meaning to them, and they in turn can be brought into the presence of the music. The attentive ear may not thereby find the solution to all its problems, but it may well succeed in throwing new light on our understanding of what Christ is saying to us at the present moment about those problems.

Such insight never comes solely through the power of intellectual activity. Thought, on its own, can get us so far, as can speech, but there comes a time *when words fail* and it is then that prayer, worship, images, myths, symbols and music have to take over, as our imagination comes into play, our awareness is heightened and our spiritual vision intensified.

Theologians and philosophers in every generation have asked the basic questions about the existence of God and whether and how it is possible for human beings to know him. Few of them seem to have paid much attention to the part which the imagination is to play in this search, perhaps because it is only in recent times that the understandings of psychology and social behaviour have been available to the enquirer. The time when we can assert quite categorically that we know **how** that imagination works may well be a long way off, which is all the more reason for trying to understand and unravel some of these fundamental problems. The paradox of not knowing by what we normally understand by the word 'knowledge', and yet knowing by faith, is one that will always be with us in this life:

> Now we see in a mirror dimly, but then face to face. Now I know in part; then I shall understand fully, even as I have been fully understood. (1 Corinthians 13.12)

It is in worship that the Christian is most likely to come nearest to this deeper knowledge of which St Paul writes, because it is the paradoxical nature of worship that we share our involvement with both God and other people:

> We cannot assume that worship is all of God, or there would be no need to add our human prayers to God's all-sufficient ones. Nor can we assume that worship is all of man, for that is the ultimate blasphemy which reduces God from an end into the means. The paradox of grace assures us that worship is hard work, requiring human effort and will. It assures it is necessary work, actually achieving something within the divine economy. Yet it reassures us that we would have no will to worship if it were not given us by God, and no effectiveness to our worship had not God designed it so.[2]

When the Godward element is allowed to disappear, the failure of worship is total. This truth is well expressed by Geoffrey Wainwright in his study on the understanding of liturgy in the light of its history:

> Worship is a human glorification of God and a divine glorification of man: in and through our giving glory to God, God himself is changing us from glory into glory.[3]

This paradox of the human and the divine elements in worship has its parallel in the experience of the Christian mystic, where at one moment it seems that God 'comes down' into the soul of the person who prays and at another it is as if the soul were 'taken up' towards God, though at no stage is there any blurring of the separate identities of the one who prays and the one to whom the prayer is offered. Rather, a mutual indwelling takes place, as is expressed in the Prayer of Humble Access, when the worshipper prepares to receive Holy Communion and prays 'that we may evermore dwell in him and he in us'.

There is a widespread feeling in the churches that the mystical path is only for the elect few. Perhaps this has come about by the way in which it has been presented, or misrepresented, or not even presented at all. It may be that there will be very few who will travel far along this particular way and most of us have neither the time nor the spiritual attrait to pursue it in any great depth, but it is high time for the myth to be exploded that 'ordinary people like us' need not concern ourselves with such exalted matters. There may well be a calling by God for some people to set out on the mystical road, especially those for whom the purely intellectual approach has been tried and found wanting. The mystical approach has to be exercised **in** the world, not as a kind of escapism **from** the world, but by bringing into it all the realities of daily life, from wet afternoons to glorious sunshine, from the people next door to the grandchildren in Sheffield.

Christians who are artists will also be involved in these tensions. Some will be doing their best to 'earth' the vision of God, perhaps by doing what artists in all ages have done, reinterpreting some scriptural incident in the idiom of today. Others will make it their task to try to lift the world above its humdrum concerns, to break out of the finitudes which govern our wordly existence. What they will not do, if they value both their spirituality and their artistic gifts, is to try to drive an artificial wedge between what they see in their contemporary world and what they believe to be beautiful: the true beauty will lie within their depiction of those things of space and time.

Another paradox concerning the earthly and the heavenly has been observed in the music of J. S. Bach, in that because 'the *St John Passion* concerns itself with the phenomenon of incarnation, it is humanistically oriented: in Jungian terminology, it concerns

God's need to become Man'. The *B minor Mass*, 'like any liturgical mass, is also about Incarnation, but approached from the opposite angle in that it concerns fallen man's need to attain to Godhead'.[4]

An interesting point is being made here, but I believe that it does less than justice to Bach, St John or the Mass if, as I understand it, the writer is suggesting that the Passion narrative in St John's Gospel is 'humanistically oriented'.

One school of theologians, those of the 'God is dead' tendency, would see all this as being completely irrelevant. Here is one of the greatest paradoxes of all, if God, the reality at the heart of all life, is no longer alive. I understand what some people who use this language are saying, and not without some justification, that some of our ideas about God must die because they are false. I have read how the most avowed of atheists, including Nietzsche and Feuerbach, have yet been completely absorbed by God. But I cannot understand how such a statement can be made: if God is dead, he is not God!

More helpful, I would suggest, is the language used by Paul Tillich in *The Courage to Be*, where he writes of the need to transcend theism in order to find the content of absolute faith, which is the 'God above God':

> The God above the God of theism is present, although hidden, in every divine-human encounter. Biblical religion as well as Protestant theology are aware of the paradoxical character of this encounter. They are aware that if God encounters man God is neither object nor subject and is therefore above the scheme into which theism has forced him .... They are aware of the paradoxical character of every prayer, of speaking to somebody to whom you cannot speak because he is not "somebody", of asking somebody of whom you cannot ask anything because he gives or gives not before you ask, of saying "thou" to somebody who is nearer to the I than the I is to itself. Each of these paradoxes drives the religious consciousness towards a God above the God of theism.[5]

When we think about God, we have to bear in mind another apparent contradiction, one which arises when we speak of him as being eternal, that is, beyond this world, with its spatial and temporal boundaries, and yet involved in its history. This is another way of saying that God is both immanent and transcendent at the same time, both totally involved in our world, through its creation, its redemption and its continuing well-being, and totally 'other' because by definition he has to be so or he would cease to be God. This well illustrates the power of paradox to juxtapose apparent contradictions and then to move beyond them into a strange and wonderful synthesis, where far more is being said than the sum of its constituent parts. As soon as the transcendent is left out, one is left with nothing more than pantheism, the belief that the universe is identical with God, and it is not too difficult to see how easy it is to transgress the line, because of our concern to maintain that God is also the God of this world.

These are not abstract concerns in terms of aesthetics: on the contrary, they are highly relevant. The poet and the painter, the dramatist and the sculptor, the architect and the musician, the novelist and the dancer all have to be involved in this world if they are to speak to it intelligibly. They cannot afford to hold so loosely to it that they lose all effective contact, yet at the same time they must have some contact with the world beyond if what they bring to us is to be an authentic revelation of the divine and not solely a creation of their devising.

The Church has a great responsibility here. It must never consciously allow itself to reject the call of God to respond to his own truth by proclaiming the truth, to his own goodness by exemplifying it in the lives of its members, and to his own beauty by striving to set before its children the truest possible reflection of that beauty. Here are some trenchant lines from Erik Routley:

> Certain phases in the controversy between the church and the artists are perplexing and astonishing to those who overhear it from outside both worlds. While at some periods the church has been a munificent patron of art, at others it seems to have carried the restraint of art to the point of a positive cult of the ugly. In this special field of music we have the whole matter in a perspective which does not apply to the other arts, since music is, among the arts, a late developer, and those periods which witnessed the church's most generous patronage of art were those in which music was still in its infancy. In a general way, we may recall what seems to be the malignant hideousness of so much nonconformist architecture in England, and the whole puritan suspicion of visual aids to worship which has conditioned so much of modern English church life. We may recall the remarkable fact that a certain kind of zeal for souls is accompanied by what sensible people regard as a debased

taste in music and ecclesiastical decor. And with all that, we must face the persistent generosity with which the church has for many generations now offered hospitality to the second-rate.[6]

Routley goes on to remind us that St Thomas Aquinas, the most notable of all the medieval scholars, has pointed to the paradox which exists within the very concept of beauty:

> It is not something existing in its own right; nor is it something having its existence wholly in the eye of the beholder, and therefore about which no general preposition can be made. Being contemplated, it pleases. It exists enough to please, but not enough to please without being contemplated.

Aquinas was writing for a world which was smaller than ours. We are aware today that there are tribes in Africa where beauty is measured by the number of rings around a girl's neck or the bones in a person's nose. We know that the Japanese geisha girl is reckoned as a paragon of beauty by the oriental eye. Neither the African tribeswoman nor the young Japanese lady would necessarily be judged as beautiful by the standard of, say, an Englishman.

Another aspect of this problem is to examine why much western art has characteristically depicted Jesus, his family and his disciples, as Europeans rather than as Palestinian Jews. It is not, I believe, a straightforward matter of xenophobia. It is more to do with our preconceived idea of what constitutes beauty: thus Chinese landscape painting is very different from that of Constable.

What artists of all cultures have in common is that, when they sit down to draw whatever is in front of them, they are searching for a truthfulness of statement, which is itself a meditative act and one in which they can (as we say) lose themselves.

★   ★   ★

Earlier in this chapter we looked at the concept of vulnerability. Through the incarnation, God humbles himself and becomes totally vulnerable by becoming man in Jesus Christ. St Paul tells us that God has exalted his Son, made him Lord of all, and given him to be our example:

Have this mind among yourselves, which is yours in Jesus Christ, who, though he was in the form of God, did not count equality with God a thing to be grasped, but emptied himself, taking the form of a servant, being born in the likeness of men. And being found in human form he humbled himself and became obedient unto death, even death on a cross. Therefore God has highly exalted him and bestowed on him the name which is above every name, that at the name of Jesus every knee should bow, in heaven and on earth and under the earth, and every tongue confess that Jesus Christ is Lord, to the glory of God the Father. (Philippians 2.5–11)

Part of this paradox stands as the great mystery which comprises the central core of the Christian faith. In his vulnerable humanity, God the Son, Jesus Christ, died on the cross 'for us and for our salvation'. In his humanity, he was raised from the dead by one of the 'mighty acts of God', the resurrection. So in the Eucharist we proclaim the mystery of faith:

Christ has died
Christ is risen
Christ will come again

Because of this, because of what Christ did and who he was, we are accepted by God not for what we have achieved, but because we are ourselves, including our weaknesses. Charles Wesley's hymn, based on the strange incident recorded in Genesis 32, where Jacob wrestled with his mysterious opponent and received his new name, Israel, recalls Paul's words, 'When I am weak, then I am strong' (2 Corinthians 12.10b):

Yield to me now, for I am weak,
But confident in self-despair;
Speak to my heart, in blessings speak,
Be conquer'd by my instant prayer!
Speak, or Thou never hence shalt move, –
And tell me, if thy Name is Love?

'Confident in self-despair': the Apostle Paul was one who lived a life which was full of contradictions, problems and paradoxes and yet, despite all the tribulations, his faith sustained him through the most appalling physical, mental and spiritual sufferings.

Here again, in words which have been a constant source of encouragement to me, he is telling us that we hold the glory of God in all its wonder and beauty within our frail humanity:

> This priceless treasure we hold, so to speak, in a common earthenware jar – to show that the splendid power of it belongs to God and not to us. We are handicapped on all sides, but we are never frustrated; we are puzzled, but never in despair. We are persecuted, but we never have to stand it alone: we may be knocked down but we are never knocked out! (2 Corinthians 4.7–9: J. B. Phillips version)

We are handicapped on all sides, but never frustrated. Each of us knows from personal experience what it is to be handicapped in some way, perhaps by illness, physical disability, anxiety or loneliness. The one thing we can never have taken from us is our spiritual freedom, which paradoxically often flourishes best in the most adverse circumstances.

We are puzzled, but never in despair. We know what it is to be bewildered, not to know what the next step should be, and very few of us reach adult life without experiencing something which we find hard to comprehend, be it illness, bereavement, doubt or the breakdown of relationships. Many have found that, at the point of deepest darkness, Christ is waiting for them.

We are persecuted, but never alone. St Paul knew better than most what this could mean and it was also to become the daily experience of the early Church, as it has been for many Christians in every age since, yet Christ himself promises that we would never be left alone: 'I am with you always, to the close of the age'. (St Matthew 28.20)

We are knocked down, but never knocked out. Like everyone else, the Christian is likely to fall. Few of us are not fighting the good fight against some temptation of the world, the flesh or the devil: we may fall, but by God's grace we get up again and continue the battle.

These paradoxes contain one of the Bible's most enduring messages of hopes. It is not only the Christian architect, writer, musician or painter who may find that these words bear a powerful message of reassurance, encouragement and salvation: they can speak with equal power and authority to each of us to accept ourselves and our circumstances as they are, yet as the prelude to change.

7 *Philosophy*

Philosophers tend to write for other philosophers: as a consequence, their ideas do not become readily available to the general reader or student. So, using the minimum necessary amount of technical language, we now examine in more detail two words which were defined briefly in Chapter 1, epistemology and aesthetics, and their relationship to one another.

Epistemology

Knowledge, the proper name for the theoretical study of which is epistemology, is something that we take for granted most of the time. But just what is knowledge and how is it possible for us to know anything? In Chapter 2 we noted three main kinds of knowledge:

(a) knowledge that, or 'factual knowledge';
(b) knowledge how, or 'practical knowledge';
(c) knowledge of, or 'knowledge by acquaintance'.

An example of factual knowledge is contained in such a statement as 'I know that the moon is about 238,857 miles from the earth'. Practical knowledge is contained in such a statement as 'She knows how to operate a word-processor'. Knowledge by acquaintance can be illustrated by my saying, 'John seems to know a lot of musicians'.

These three ways of knowing must now be supplemented by two others, since this will enable us to take the next step, which is to discover how we can know God.

The first is something which goes beyond what is possible to know by the direct use of our powers of reasoning and understanding, as when we have some flash of illumination which immediately, and as if from nowhere, lights up something which has been in our minds. We usually call this kind of knowing **intuitive knowledge** and we often think of it as something with which women are specially gifted, though it is by no means an exclusively feminine trait. It is very much what I would associate with William Wordsworth, the poet, and William Blake, the visionary. Whilst it must be accepted that all manner of influences, conscious or subconscious, make their contribution to this way of knowing, it is nevertheless sufficiently independent of the other three to merit a category of its own.

The second way of knowing, which has been touched on several times already in this book, is **mystical knowledge**, the insight gained from the contemplation of God, chiefly through prayer, but in many other ways as well. The *Oxford Dictionary of the Christian Church* actually recognises mysticism as a separate kind of knowing by defining it as an 'immediate knowledge of God attained in this present life through personal religious experience'.

If we are concerned with knowledge, and in particular with the knowledge of God, we must at the same time be concerned with the related issues of faith and doubt, of certainty and possibility. Once we start using statements such as 'I know that there is a God', we should be prepared to bring forward the evidence for it. Either our reason tells us that this must be true, or our experience tells us that it is true because, in our communing with Jesus Christ, we have become aware not only that God is, but also that we are able to have a personal knowledge of him through prayer.

We ourselves are creatures of God, so there should be no great surprise that this kind of knowledge is possible if he has oriented us in such a way that we are able to know him through our spirituality. The combination of knowing ourselves, or being self-conscious, and knowing everything which is outside ourselves, embraces the possibility that we can know the God who gives us our personal self-awareness and our awareness of the personality of other people. Philosophers in general are not prepared to make any definitive statements about God: anything which strays into the realm of metaphysics is automatically regarded with deep suspicion. The only way of validating such statements as we have been considering (e.g. 'I know God') is by examining the source of such claims. This is likely to prove so subjective a business that we have to fall back on looking at their outcome in terms of the life lived by the claimant: 'You will know them by their fruits', says Jesus (St Matthew 7.20). This, of course, is moving us into the realm of faith, which leads us to assert our knowledge of God through our belief in his existence. This may then be followed up by trusting him with our lives.

Imagination

An important link between epistemology and aesthetics is that mental faculty which we all possess to a greater or lesser degree, imagination. It would be a serious mistake to dismiss our imagination as no more than the ability to picture familiar things in our minds, so as to create a fantasy world for temporary habitation. The Romantic poets, for example, were well aware of the distinction between 'Fancy' and 'Imagination'. If we had no imagination at all we would be hard put to have any understanding whatsoever of our surroundings. It is the creative use of the mind with which we are concerned here, as when the artist paints a picture, the poet writes a verse, or the musician composes a melody. The imaginative faculty is likewise employed at the other end of the process, as the viewer looks at the picture, the reader studies the verse or the hearer listens to the music. Again, it is the imagination which is being used when the person at prayer contemplates God.

The eighteenth-century German philosopher, Immanuel Kant, devoted much of his life to the understanding of knowledge and was incidentally no supporter of the traditional 'proofs' for the existence of God. In his working out of the principles which govern thought and knowledge, he recognised the importance of the imagination as a linking factor between what goes on in our thinking *processes* and what we are thinking about. When we are thinking about God, the same imagination is being used, not some other hidden faculty. Furthermore, it operates of necessity in that world of images and symbols which we looked at earlier.

It is in part this gift of imagination which enables us to appreciate the things of beauty in God's creation, both in this world and beyond.

Aesthetics

Aesthetics, as the word is used today, is defined as the philosophical study of beauty in art, with particular reference to the creation of what is beautiful by artists working in many different fields, and the perception of it in the experience of the viewer or listener. It also concerns itself with such questions as the criteria for determining what actually constitutes a work of art, with the theories of art, and with theoretical studies of meaning in art. In its original Greek usage, it covered a slightly different area, namely any material thing which can be perceived by our natural senses. Under the

influence of the eighteenth-century philosopher, Alexander
Gottlieb Baumgarten (1714–1762), it took on its modern significance as the study of beauty, in nature as well as in art. Von
Balthasar tells us that in the days before Baumgarten and Kant,
aesthetics was an aspect of metaphysics:

> Metaphysics was the science concerned with the being of what
> exists and, in so far as by "being" was meant that which finally
> establishes the multiplicity of the world, metaphysics was insepa-
> rable from theology. On such a view ... the beauty that blazes forth
> in single acts of appearing was anchored in an absolute beauty that
> does not pass away, a beauty that dwells ... with the "divine", with
> "God".[1]

Beauty

The word 'beauty' also deserves further explanation, even though
we have our own ideas as to what constitutes it. The subjective
element is extremely important, so long as we remember that our
own feelings are not always reliable guides and that other people's
views may be entirely different from our own.

One dictionary of philosophy defines beauty somewhat
narrowly as the 'property of an object giving rise to pleasure or
approval, the latter requiring justification in terms of the characteristics of the object'.[2] Another prefers 'the sensible condition of
aesthetic excellence considered to arouse the keenest pleasure'. It
points out that the concepts of art and creativity have largely
replaced the word 'beauty'.[3]

What has been lost with this shift of meaning in relatively recent
timed is the natural relationship that exits between theology and
art, both of which are concerned with beauty, the one chiefly with
the beauty of God, the other with the beauty of human creativity.
Any Christian theology which leaves out all aesthetic considerations is a defective theology, for at the centre of its study should be
the ultimate in beauty, God himself. Writing in a book on sculpture, H. von Zeller draws a distinction between absolute and relative beauty:

> While every object of beauty that results from the work of man
> is a reflection of God's absolute beauty, those objects which are
> called religious and Christian must reflect God's beauty in a
> particular way.

If it is to qualify as a work of sacred art, then, the object must be directed: ultimately towards God, immediately towards the service of religion. If it is further to qualify as beautiful, it must reveal a concern more with absolute than with relative beauty.[4]

This begs the question of how one can either define or reflect the beauty of God. One can see the beauty of God's creation and one can praise him for it, but that does not thereby enable us to visualize his beauty *per se*.

In addition, it is unwise to consider beauty in isolation from the other transcendentals, even though it may be convenient at times to give particular attention to it, for truth and goodness are really inseparable from beauty. They form a triad of values comparable in their unity to the three great theological virtues, faith, hope and love.

★   ★   ★

In the light of these definitions, we can now look again at various forms and see how it is possible to assess them in terms of both their beauty and our perception of them.

Art defies easy definition even though we are all aware of its existence. The last few decades have seen a general broadening of the popular conception of what actually constitutes art: for example, our Edwardian forbears would be surprised if they could hear us discussing photography, the cinema and television as art forms. Hans Küng uses very strong language to point to the distinction between the meaning and the purpose of a work of art:

Genuine art has a meaning, something that justifies the work of art in itself; but art as such has no purpose or use. Indeed, a work of art designed. to be useful or to serve certain interests is a betrayal of art.[5]

Although this calls into question the entire use of art by Christians as a didactic device, few Christians would question that you cannot readily separate art from religion or, for that matter, from any other aspect of life. Where art has become debased it can often be put down to the materialism of the age in which we live and its consequent detachment from the values which Christianity asserts and maintains. Where art is at its truest, there will always be those willing to acknowledge its rightness and its beauty and to see behind it and through it the God of beauty and order.

Over the five year period between 1908 and 1913, the Dutch painter, Piet Mondrian (1872–1944), contemplated a tree and painted it over and over again until, in the end, he felt that the only truthful way to describe that tree was by abstracting it into an order of different geometric shapes. In so doing, he:

> "rediscovered the primordial significance of the vertical and hori-
> zontal, a significance which is known to traditional man through the
> cosmic symbolism of weaving, where the union of warp and weft
> symbolizes the union of all the opposites (heaven and earth, etc.)
> upon which the fabric of existence is woven ... Through a long
> process of refinement and distillation the outer image of the trees
> gradually dissolves, finally disappearing altogether. What remains are
> its vertical and horizontal axes, the warp and weft out of which exis-
> tence is woven and sustained." [6]

Ben Nicholson (1894–1982) is another of the many artists who have ended up painting geometry because this was the only way they could give their full respect to the order and perfection of creation. I have in mind particularly his Still Life and Painted Relief works in oil and pencil, executed between 1935 and 1945.

As art itself is constantly on the move and exploring new frontiers of creation, so the aesthetic response of each new generation will experience changes, often subtle and gradual, sometimes sudden and traumatic, with standards for judging art constantly on the move.

★   ★   ★

Architecture is the most distinctively visible of all the art forms and one from which escape is almost impossible. The responsibility of the architect is to design a building which fulfils its necessary func-tions and to do it with such good taste that it is itself aesthetically pleasing and that it sits happily in its surroundings. The architect will have to consider how to incorporate all the practical features that are required of a school, hospital, church, shop, or whatever, as well as having an eye to its inherent beauty, in terms of design, materials and siting. To what degree he is successful will be judged by both those who use the building and those who merely see it.

Value judgements such as these are applied, *mutatis mutandis*, to all forms of art and it is not always the artist who has got it right. The person on the top of the bus may have little or no technical expertise, but may well have an exceedingly well-developed aesthetic sense which knows almost intuitively when something is wrong by being out of scale, out of place, out of sympathy, or out of proportion.

Let us take, as an example, the architecture of railways, forever associated with names such as Tite, Scott, Mocatta and Cubitt. Think of the enormous variety of building types and styles, from 'Gothic' London terminus to 'Classical' roundhouse, together with a wide assortment of bridges, viaducts, warehouses, and even entire towns and villages. It is not difficult to understand how readily comparisons are made between humble wayside stations and tiny mission chapels; between stately town stations and major parish churches; and above all between the principal termini and the great cathedrals of our land. Here is David Atwell on London's Paddington Station:

> Brunel's vision was of a vast, glazed, aisled cathedral. Cast iron columns support a gigantic triple roof where every third arched rib rests directly on a slender octagonal pier, the intermediate ones on open cross members; the "nave" is 102 feet wide and the "aisles" 70 feet and 68 feet respectively; and there are two pairs of unique "transepts" along the sides.[7]

Usually when we travel by train we take little note of the architecture of the railways, yet a keen, if unprofessional, eye will quickly detect what is 'right' and what is 'wrong'.

Every generation in which there is vitality, drive and inventiveness will be creating new norms of what it believes to be beautiful and will express this most evidently in the buildings it creates, be they hideous 1960s tower blocks, ornate Victorian railway stations or medieval cathedrals. All of them will testify to the contemporary philosophy of beauty and will have an important aesthetic message, whether positive or negative.

*   *   *

We are probably almost as judgemental in our attitude to literature as we are to architecture, as witness such statements as, It doesn't rhyme, it doesn't scan, so it isn't poetry'. What is it that we are judging when we express our opinions? First we are passing a verdict on the content, as we seek to answer such questions as, 'What was it about? Was it a good story? Were there memorable images in the poem? Was what was written for the stage dramatically satisfying?' Secondly we are judging the style, again by answering questions such as, 'What was the sentence construction like? Were poetic images well put across in the balance of lines and verse? Were the acting and the staging of the play satisfactory?'

These sets of questions are ultimately aesthetic ones because they assess the beauty of the work as a whole and in its details in terms of content and style. They will help us to come to our own understanding of whether or not it was good literature but the Christian will probably wish to go on to explore the theological dimension as well. This does not mean that we can only make a proper aesthetic assessment if we are trained theologians, but rather to ask a further series of questions along the lines of, 'Was what I read or heard good or bad from the point of view of the behaviour of the characters in it and was it true to the Christian revelation of truth, in so far as it had any specifically religious content?'

★   ★   ★

A different set of questions will be in our minds when we listen to music, but the same underlying concerns will be present for the aesthetic integrity of the composition and its performance. This, of all the arts, is the one which gives most meaning to the title of this book, because the language of music is totally different from that of our speech and possesses a unique ability to take us onwards from the point *when words fail*. There is something peculiarly appropriate about music that enables it to convey a quality of spirituality specially suitable for worship. There is a potential problem lurking here for those who are responsible for the selection and performance of music in a liturgical context. Should we ever use music which is less than fitting from the aesthetic standpoint as part of a church service? The answer, in all honesty, should be 'No', but there cannot be many clergy or organists who have not, from time to time, chosen an inferior tune for a well-known hymn on the sole ground that it will be better known to the congregation.

Here we have an interesting conflict between what may be pastorally appropriate and what is aesthetically right, though we can at least make an occasional attempt to introduce our congregations to new music. I think, for example, of the new enthusiasm of a congregation for singing Newman's words, 'Lead, kindly light' when they realise that there is a superb tune, *Alberta*, by William Harris in place of the dirge, *Sandon*, by C. H. Purday. Much the same is true of Vaughan Williams' tune *Kingsfold* for 'I heard the voice of Jesus say', instead of the well-loved but musically insignificant *Vox Dilecti* by J. B. Dykes.

The majority of the world's truly great composers have moved with apparently effortless ease between the 'sacred' and the 'secular', providing music for the liturgy one day, for the orchestra the next and for the opera the day after. Much of it, and not only the church music, is an expression of true beauty. Some of it, especially that of Bach and Mozart, is generally recognized as being to all intents and purposes aesthetically perfect.

8 *Partnership*

Were it not for the careful and diligent observation and meticulous recording of Dr John Watson we would never have heard of the amazing powers of deduction of that celebrated resident of number 221b Baker Street, London, Mr Sherlock Holmes. Lost to humanity would have been the extraordinary adventures of those two men as described in *The Hound of the Baskervilles* and *The Speckled Band*.

This fictional partnership, so memorably created by Sir Arthur Conan Doyle, can be matched by many factual ones. No one would have imagined that, when a musician called Arthur Sullivan and a poet named William Gilbert began to collaborate on some works of light operatic comedy, their labours would have given such delight to millions of people all over the world for the next century and more.

Who would have guessed that the stall in the open market in Leeds established in 1884 by two such unlikely partners as the Jewish refugee from Poland, Michael Marks, and the business partner whom he took on in 1894, Thomas Spencer, would one day become an international multi-million pound empire and a household name?

Partnerships of one kind or another are in evidence in every sphere of life. Beyond all the lesser ones of family, social, church and business life stands the partnership between God and his creation, of which the summit is humanity. Beyond that again is the perfect partnership within the Godhead, of Father, Son and Holy Spirit, that Trinity of equal Beings, three Persons in one God.

Our human partnerships are naturally of very great significance to us because they help to express our nature as social beings, sharing different aspects of our life with other people, whether in love or friendship, work or sport. This last aspect of our community life is of immense importance, judging by the number of people involved in it as participants or spectators on a Saturday afternoon. Unless we are out-and-out loners, we enjoy being members or supporters of a team and no small part of our education and training in life is directed towards this end. In our social life, the origins of the word 'companionship' are concerned with sharing, the sharing of our food (Latin: *con*=with; *panis*=bread).

It is through partnership, formal or informal, that much of the mutual service which is vital to the life of the community is expressed, whether the banding together of a small group to form a Victim Support Scheme in their neighbourhood or the international organisations which enable countries to work together for the common good, such as the British Commonwealth or the United Nations Organisation.

In this chapter we take up the theme of partnership and assess its working in the world of aesthetics. The partnership between religion and literature is considerably less in evidence today than it was even two or three generations ago. Among the reasons for this must clearly be the general decline in religion as a natural part of our way of life, and as such the natural subject matter for the story-teller's art. Because much of the earliest literature of the world was of a religious nature, literature and religion served to record, illuminate and interpret one another.

The Judaeo-Christian literary heritage is an extremely rich one and includes not only straightforward stories, but also myth and history, poetry and wisdom, prophecy and law, whilst the four Gospels of the New Testament form an entirely new literary genre in themselves. The nineteen centuries since have been rich with Christian literature in the form of history (the Venerable Bede and Owen Chadwick); poetry (George Herbert and Ruth Pitter); drama (the anonymous writers of the mystery plays and Dorothy L. Sayers); novels (Charles Williams and Graham Greene); apologists (Richard Hooker and C. S. Lewis) and so on; and the names in brackets, only from our own land, are simply by way of illustrations and could be multiplied many times over.

The two great themes of all Christian literature are the relationship of the soul to God and the inter-relationship of human beings, of which the latter is most clearly portrayed in the form of the novel. I would not wish to imply that all literature is religious, but a considerable amount of religious writing today comes from the pens of those who would not specifically call themselves religious, let alone Christian. They seek to grapple with questions that are at heart religious questions, because they concern all the experiences of life as well as those things which have a more obvious connection with God.

Because I have much enjoyed them myself, I would like to use the works of four writers of English fiction, one from each of the last four centuries, to illustrate the way in which different authors of different periods have addressed this theme. Readers will of course realise that such a choice is highly selective and that poets and playwrights, too, have much to say to us in this respect. Each of these writers has developed in his works the relationship between God and individual people and that between one person and another.

John Bunyan (1628–1688) would not have claimed to be a novelist, though he stands head and shoulders above all the other writers of fiction of his century. He was, at different times in his life, tinsmith, soldier, husband, nonconformist preacher, prisoner, writer and mystic. His twelve years in prison were the result not of criminal behaviour as we would understand it today but of his refusal to toe the Anglican line at a time when failure to do so brought one up against the stiff penal laws which were introduced at the time of the Restoration of the Monarchy in 1660. His early devotional works were of little lasting significance but served to prepare him for his first major success, *Grace Abounding* (1666), a spiritual autobiography written half-way through his first imprisonment.

Bunyan is chiefly remembered for another work, started during his last imprisonment in Bedford Gaol and published in two parts (1678 and 1684) with the immortal title, *The Pilgrim's Progress*, an allegorical story of the journey of life, with its memorable characterisations of such people as Christian, Mr Worldly Wiseman, Mr Good-will and Faithful, together with such landmarks on the journey as the Slough of Despond, the Wicket-Gate, the Celestial City and Vanity Fair.

In these and in the two other major works which followed, *The Life and Death of Mr Badman* (1680) and *The Holy War* (1682), his great success is largely attributable to a combination of three factors. First, there is his natural writing talent and down-to-earthness; next, the view widely accepted by him and his contemporaries that there exists a clear line between those chosen by God and those rejected by him; and then the mystical quality which these had helped to form within him.

Oliver Goldsmith (c.1728–1784) lived precisely a century later than Bunyan and used his poetic skills to portray some of the problems of his day, both in his native Ireland and in England, problems brought about by the contemporary economic and social malaise. This he did most strikingly in *The Traveller* (1764) and *The Deserted Village* (1770), whilst his 1773 comedy-drama, *She Stoops to Conquer*, has stood the test of well over two centuries of performance. Samuel Johnson was to say of him that he worked in every literary field and was an adornment to each.

Not surprisingly for a man who had been brought up in a parsonage house, success as a novelist came with the publication in 1766 of his only work in that genre, *The Vicar of Wakefield*, though with his medical training he could perhaps as easily have written an equally sympathetic study of a devoted general practitioner. Despite its obvious improbabilities and implausibilities, the story of Dr Primrose is gracefully told and the eponymous pastor comes across as a simple yet effective servant of God.

Sir Walter Scott, in his life of Goldsmith, writes with warm approval of this novel and its author, that:

> (he) wrote to exalt virtue and expose vice; and he accomplished his task in a manner which raises him to the highest rank among British authors.[1]

Charles Kingsley (1819–1875), though like Goldsmith the son of a clergyman and a man with a mission to reform social evils, came from a somewhat different background and was strongly influenced by his friendship with F. D. Maurice, one of the founders of the Christian Socialist movement. After studying at King's College, London and at Magdalene College, Cambridge, he moved to Hampshire and passed most of his life as vicar of Eversley, where he gained a reputation as an opponent of asceticism and a proponent of 'Muscular Christianity'. His principal novels were *Alton Locke* (1850), *Yeast* (1851), *Hypatia* (1853, his own favourite), *Westward Ho!* (1855, his most famous), *The Heroes* (1856), *The Water Babies* (1863) and *Hereward the Wake* (1865).

Much of his writing is directed to the cause of social reform, an objective which was to be brought about not by violence or rebellion, but by the persuasive power of moral force. Right from the start, in *Alton Locke* and *Yeast*, he paints a forceful portrait of the misery endured by the hundreds of thousands who were forced to work in conditions of appalling squalor, either in factories or on the land. *Hypatia*, set in fifth-century Alexandria, is an historical novel about power and corruption in the Christian Church, whilst *The Water Babies* is a fantasy for children which touches on the theme of social justice right from its opening paragraph. It describes the illiterate, unwashed and hungry little chimney-sweep, Tom, who has 'to climb the dark flues, rubbing his poor knees and elbows raw', and who is beaten at regular intervals by his master.

The Australian writer, **Morris West**, uses his own experience as a teaching monk to fix the Christian Church in the centre of nearly all his novels. In most of them there is a social gospel to proclaim as well as a spiritual one. In *Children of the Sun*, he exposes the desperate plight of children growing up in the slums of Naples, with all their concomitant dirt, starvation and emotional deprivation. In *The Devil's Advocate*, the story of Blaise Meredith, a Roman Catholic priest who has to enquire into the life of a popular hero who is being considered for canonisation, he writes perceptively about some of the darker aspects of the human condition and explores what he himself calls 'the contrasts between the human and the divine elements in Christian beliefs'.

The Shoes of the Fisherman, his best-known novel, covers the election conclave and early months in office of Kiril Cardinal Lakota, a Pope of the twentieth-century, who writes in his secret diary that:

> the mystery of evil is the deepest one of all. It is the mystery of the primal creative act, when God called into existence the human soul, made in His own image, and presented it with the terrifying choice, to centre upon itself, or to centre itself upon Him without whom it could not subsist at all.

In *The Clowns of God*, West has another modern Pope abdicating after claiming to have received a personal revelation of the Second Coming of Christ. With deep spiritual insight and dramatic skill he depicts man as:

> a creature who walks in two worlds and traces upon the walls of his cave the wonders and the nightmare experiences of his personal pilgrimage.

Such a selection clearly cannot do justice to the great contribution which literature has made to our understanding of the religious questions raised by the relationship of man to his maker and to his fellows, but they may serve as indicators that the novelist can often open our minds to a deeper comprehension of these mysteries, in much the same way as poets or dramatists can through their particular craft.

★   ★   ★

Because fewer people come into contact with painting and sculpture, the public profile of those two art forms is considerably lower than that of literature yet they, too, witness to the partnership between art and religion and between the artist and the viewer. With sculpture there is the additional relationship between the sculptor and the material on which he is working and with which he is seeking to express some aspect of life. The once strong partnership between the church and the sculptor exists today only in a very attenuated form: shortage of money for commissioning new work is one reason, a general lack of interest in sculpture is another, and the general decline in concern for the things of the spirit is a third. It is factors such as these which make the last work of Elizabeth Frink (1930–1993) for Liverpool Cathedral so significant.

Painting faces a similar dissolution of a long-standing relationship and for much the same reasons. This makes it all the more important that the artist should maintain his or her artistic integrity when faced with the temptation to produce something which may be popular and relatively inexpensive but which does damage to the artist's own spirit by not being an honest response of mind and soul to the creative challenge. It is not overstating the case to talk about a crisis in the partnership between the arts and the Christian faith and it is realistic to assume that there will be no speedy resolution of it as long as humanity as a whole rejects religious standards and values.

We have noted already that the judgement of a work of art is a two-way process, with the viewer being judged by the painting as well as the more obvious judgement of the painting by the beholder. What the viewer sees and how he or she responds to it is what forms the ultimate valuation of the work itself. It is almost irrelevant that what moves one person leaves another untouched, what is dull to one is exquisite to another. We must each come to our own decision, based as it will be on many factors, some of which will be rising up from layers of thought well below the conscious, through processes of which we are not even aware.

The more aware we are of our personal prejudices, the more we can discount them. The work of art can then speak for itself without undue hindrance, especially to those whose appreciation of art has been nourished along fairly traditional lines and who now find themselves confronted by work in an unfamiliar modern idiom, an experience which can be extremely disconcerting. Our whole approach will be much more balanced and open if we bear in mind that the artist is saying something to us about his or her vision of the world and trying to communicate this to us through the use of appropriate materials, shapes, colours and symbols.

Much depends on how, if at all, we have learnt to interpret art. Eric Kennington (1888–1960) went into the desert to draw his superb paintings of the Arabs who had taken part in T. E. Lawrence's campaign during the First World War, drawings which were used to illustrate *Seven Pillars of Wisdom*. Amazingly to us, the Arabs to whom they were shown were unable to interpret them because they had never seen a reproduction of the three-dimensional world on a two-dimensional sheet of paper. This is something we are doing all the time, without even thinking about it: we take it for granted and base our aesthetic judgements on it. If we are unfamiliar with the language, we shall be incapable of making a proper judgement of the quality of what we see.

There are times when the artist will be exercising a priestly function, by standing 'on the Godward side of man', to receive a vision of what is truly beautiful and to make this visible to us through the chosen medium. This action, however, always has to take place within the setting of the contemporary world and there is therefore an inalienable partnership between art and society as well as between art and religion. For all his or her journeys into the sublime, the artist remains neither more nor less than a human being, who must somehow translate the vision of the divine into something to which other human beings can respond. This will be equally true whether the work is overtly inspired by religion (as, for example, a scene from the life of Jesus) or whether it has no specifically Christian reference, and is therefore a testimony in the wider sense to the creative ability which is the gift of God.

★   ★   ★

As artists of a different kind, musicians share some of the same functions as painters, bringing to us a revelation of beauty which would otherwise be inaccessible, through a God-given ability to translate the vision of what is lovely into a language which, though it is without words, is nevertheless intelligible to the human mind and resonates within the human heart. It is what we make of the sounds we hear, filtered through the whole of our background and experience of life, which is what ultimately counts, rather than what the music critic tells us. There is nothing to stop our bene-fitting from what the critics say, because their education and training may well make them more aware than we are of the deeper message of the music, its construction, its language, and its interpretation, all of which help us to a more profound experience than might otherwise have been possible.

Our aesthetic sensibility is unlikely to stand still for long unless we deliberately choose to fossilize it at a particular stage of its development, and even that would not be easy. The more trouble we take to understand what we hear, the more likely it is that our understanding will deepen, though we have to be careful that we do not become musical snobs in the process: that, needless to say, applies to any form of aesthetic experience and not only to music.

★   ★   ★

There is another interesting example of partnership in our use of the word 'church', which in one context signifies the people of God and in another context refers to a building. There is an important link between the two because they are by no means in opposition to one another but are different aspects of the same theological concept. In the vision of Jacob at Bethel, already described in Chapter 3, we read how Jacob awoke from his sleep and said:

> How awesome is this place! This is none other than the house of God, and this is the gate of heaven. (Genesis 28.17)

That phrase, 'house of God', has become a regular part of our Christian vocabulary and is one of the most expressive terms that we can use to designate a church building. As Christ became man and was 'tabernacled' among us, so we set aside our churches as the places (but not the only places) where the glorified Lord comes once again to his people, when the gate of heaven is opened in the Eucharist.

Another heavenly vision is given to man in the Apocalypse, but now there is no need for any house of God in the form of a building:

> I saw no temple in the city, for its temple is the Lord God the Almighty and the Lamb. And the city has no need for sun or moon to shine upon it, for the glory of God is its light, and its lamp is the Lamb. (Revelation 21.22–23)

Meanwhile, back on earth, we still need our churches, chapels and cathedrals as the focal points for the gathering of the Christian community around the twin symbols of the reality of God's presence, the book and the table, the Bible and the Altar. How impressive it is to see the Benedictine monks of a French abbey revering the Word of God in scripture in the same way as they revere the Word made flesh in the Eucharist, by affording to each a profound bow and, after the reading of the Gospel, holding up the Bible and calling for the Word of God to be acclaimed.

Because this balance is theologically sound, it needs to be expressed as clearly as possible in the design and construction of our churches, so that the people of God are centring their devotion on the book and the table, and are seen to be doing so and enabled to do so. The central importance of this partnership of Word and Sacrament within the fellowship of the Church, its 'koinonia', to use St Paul's word, needs to be reflected in their being set in an environment which is as aesthetically sensitive as possible.

When we worship, we are making a statement about what we believe, not a straightforward credal affirmation such as is often said or sung during a church service, but a more subtle, even subconscious, declaration of our understanding of God. This is conveyed in part by the actual words we use, many of which will have been chosen for us by a particular prayer book and a particular lectionary, and in part by the way in which the worship is conducted and shared. Considerable responsibility, therefore, rests on the shoulders of clergy and ministers and all others involved in leadership roles, together with their congregations, to ensure that the right signals are being transmitted and received.

Following the example of the Roman Catholic Church, many other Christians have acquired the habit of asserting that they are the 'Easter People', believers in, and witnesses to, the resurrection of Jesus Christ. This means that our worship as well as our lives will express the conviction that in Christ we are given a newness of life which is obtainable from no other source. Where something of this glory fails to break through and illuminate and energize our worship, there is something amiss with the life of the Christian community and its leaders.

Another liturgical partnership which should not be overlooked is the one which exists between the Church of today and the Church of the past. Constantly in our worship we draw on the deep well of the resources of Christian experience: our readings from holy scripture take us back to the earliest days of the Church and, in the case of the Old Testament, well beyond. Some of our prayers and liturgies have their origins in the earliest centuries of the Church's life. Our hymns are an amazing collection of devotion spanning many centuries and cultures. The buildings in which we worship are part of an exceedingly rich heritage stretching back well over a thousand years. All these contributions from the past should not be allowed to overwhelm the contemporary setting and the contemporary experience of the Church's faith, which will be reflected in the use of today's prayers and music in buildings which are either designed or adapted for today's liturgical needs, and enriched by today's artistry.

This does not mean that the Church has to adopt every passing trend and fancy. What it does mean is that those in positions of responsibility and leadership should be aware of the contemporary movements in liturgy, language, culture and art, and be willing to learn what is really good in them and which of them are aesthetically right. This is particularly true when it comes to the partnership between language and worship. The language of liturgy should never be allowed to become completely sterile or fossilized and should always be consonant with the message it conveys, taking note of contemporary usage but not falling below the appropriate thresholds of grammar, vocabulary and rhythm. As an example of good modern liturgical writing one could cite the first of the two post-communion prayers in Rite A of The Alternative Service Book 1980:

> Father of all, we give you thanks and praise, that when we were still far off you met us in your Son and brought us home. Dying and living, he declared your love, gave us grace, and opened the gate of glory. May we who share Christ's body live his risen life; we who drink his cup bring life to others; we whom the Spirit lights give light to the world. Keep us firm in the hope you have set before us, so we and all your children shall be free, and the whole earth live to praise your name; through Christ our Lord. Amen.

Not only does this say what needs to be said in terms of thanksgiving, memorial and future aspiration, but it does so in simple words within short sentences, and using a wealth of poetic imagery.

How we pray in private is a totally different matter because the actual words we use can be completely informal, even unstructured. The aesthetic value of this kind of prayer lies much more in the natural beauty of the conversation of the soul with its maker, which may not be dependent on words at all. When we begin as learners in the school of prayer, we may find that forms of prayer are provided for us from the earliest days we can remember. As we progress with age and experience, we may still wish to continue with such childlike simplicity and directness but at the same time to broaden the scope of our prayer to include more than straightforward intercession and to deepen it by the inclusion of other elements, such as the adoration of God, thanksgiving, and confession of our personal sins and shortcomings. Each of these forms of prayer is an expression of that partnership which we have with God through our awareness of the fact of his own being, his generosity as giver of all good things and the assurance of his forgiving love, of which the sign and symbol is the crucified Christ.

★　　★　　★

I want to close this chapter with two further illustrations of the theme of partnership. First, there is a close relationship between our knowledge of God and our knowledge of other people. The writer of a New Testament Epistle from which I have already quoted is pretty scathing about those who claim to have a partnership with God, yet refuse to acknowledge that which already exist with their fellows:

> If anyone says, "I love God," and hates his brother, he is a liar; for he who does not love his brother whom he has seen, cannot love God whom he has not seen. And this commandment we have from him that he who loves God should love his brother also. (1 John 4.20–21)

Without this partnership with our fellow human beings we cannot hope to attain to any real partnership with our Father in heaven.

Secondly, there is that link between theology and imagination which we have already noted. That partnership has not always enjoyed a good press, especially when it has got into the hands of those whose special study is the working of the human mind: the psychiatrist, the psychotherapist, the clinical psychologist. This certainly does not mean that we are to abandon all claims to any such partnership. Instead, we need to look at it again, critically reasserting our awareness of the possibility of self-delusion yet stressing that imagination *is* a God-given faculty, part of the human psyche, and thus an important element in our attempt to know God, either directly or through the beauty which he has manifested in the natural world, in human creativity and in human relationships.

9 *Prayer*

It is probably through prayer, private or public, spoken or silent, that people have come to know God more than through any other way, not excluding nature and scripture, though the Bible has given us many of our most treasured insights into the nature of the God to whom we pray and can be a powerful adjunct to prayer.

The links between prayer and aesthetics are plentiful, with architecture forming the setting for much of our common prayer, music being its natural accompaniment, painting and sculpture serving often as its silent witnesses, and literature of one kind or another being its outward and audible sign.

We have already seen how crucial for a proper performance of the liturgy is a right understanding of the relationship between the building itself and what goes on inside it, a theme to which we will return in Chapter 12. For the moment, we need to bear in mind that a church building exists, before all other purposes, to provide a spiritual home for the local worshipping community. In the middle ages, our churches and cathedrals did much more than this: today they may still be centres of pilgrimage, concert halls, meeting places, or glorious pieces of architecture which people come to admire for their aesthetic splendour. All those are by-products, incidental to the main purpose: if their regular congregations cannot pray in them, the other things may still happen but the buildings will not be fulfilling their proper role.

Where the liturgy is deformed by the failure to recognise and abide by good theological principles, it becomes that much less a proper vehicle for the apprehension of the reality of God by the worshipper. This is another of those cases where truth and beauty go hand in hand, for our worship is one of the most accurate barometers of our understanding of God and will inevitably be a reflection of it. Thus bad theology leads to bad liturgy: we cannot expect to hear God speaking clearly to us if we approach him in words and actions which do him less than justice.

An article by Michael Vasey on the Church's role in worship sums up the main liturgical principles of Thomas Cranmer, the prime inspirer of the Book of Common Prayer, principles which are equally valid today and which find renewed expression in The Alternative Service Book 1980 of the Church of England:

> *First*, worship should be biblical in the doctrine it expresses, should familiarise worshippers with the content of scripture and should draw on the imagery and ideas of the bible.

> *Second*, worship should be adapted to the language, customs and circumstances of the worshippers.

> *Third*, where it is possible and helpful, worship should continue the customs and traditions of the ancient Church.

> *Fourth*, worship should be the ordered, reverent, corporate activity of the whole Church of Christ, clergy and people together.[1]

Cranmer would surely have been amazed to know that his work had lasted for nearly 450 years, albeit with certain official and unofficial revisions, as no doubt would be the revisers of his work who compiled the Prayer Book of 1662, and who declared their belief that no liturgy should become so unchanging and unchanged that it could no longer be a worthy mode of worship for those who used it. Here are their words from the Preface of 1662, drafted by Robert Sanderson, Bishop of Lincoln:

> It hath been the wisdom of the Church of *England*, ever since the first compiling of her Publick Liturgy to keep the mean between the two extremes, of too much stiffness in refusing, and of too much easiness in admitting any variation from it. For, as on the one side common experience sheweth, that where a change hath been made of things advisedly established (no evident necessity so requiring) sundry inconveniences have thereupon ensued; and those many times more and greater than the evils, that were intended to be remedied by such change: So on the other side, the particular Forms of Divine worship, and the Rites and Ceremonies appointed to be used therein, being things in their own nature indifferent, and alterable, and so acknowledged; it is but reasonable, that upon weighty and important considerations, according to the various exigency of times and occasions, such changes and alterations should be made therein, as to those that are in place of Authority should from time to time seem either necessary or expedient.

It is instructive to set these words alongside Archbishop John Habgood's Preface to the ASB:

The Church of England has traditionally sought to maintain a balance between the old and the new. For the first time since the Act of Uniformity this balance in its public worship is now officially expressed in two books, rather than in one. The Alternative Service Book (1980), as its name implies, is intended to supplement the Book of Common Prayer, not to supersede it. The addition of a date to its title may serve as a reminder that revision and adaptation of the Church's worship are continuous processes, and that any liturgy, no matter how timeless its qualities, also belongs to a particular period and culture.

Here we find something of a paradox. Yes, the structure and language of worship do change and must change, though too many changes occurring too quickly leave a congregation lost and bewildered in a liturgical landscape without any familiar reference points. Because it takes time for a new liturgy to become accepted, a sudden revolution is likely to be counterproductive. The ASB has enjoyed its warmest welcome in those places and among those congregations which have experienced a gradual transition from the Book of Common Prayer. Series 1 and 2 of the 1960s prepared the way by restoring the shape of the liturgy to its earlier form but maintaining much of the traditional language, especially the thee/thou/thy form of address to God. Series 3 of the 1970s was written in the you/your idiom and began to introduce worshippers to a more flexible form of service.

The ASB of 1980 consolidated the fruits of these experiments into one book which then provided the Church of England with three legal eucharistic liturgies, each containing its own permissible variants. Rite A, with its choice of four eucharistic prayers, provides the order which incorporates the most radical changes from what had hitherto been customary. Rite B also allows considerable flexibility whilst maintaining the more traditional linguistic structures. The order of the Book of Common Prayer also still remains in use, even though it is probably never celebrated precisely according to its own rubrics.

In each of these forms of worship – and the story is paralleled in other branches of the Christian Church – the intention is that of the Psalmist, 'to behold the fair beauty of the Lord', and this is done by presenting him, in word and sacrament, as the perfect revelation of God's beauty – incarnate, crucified, dead, risen, ascended, and now proclaimed as Lord of all.

John Fenton, in an article in the *Church Times* on October 9th, 1992 provides us with a helpful definition of good and bad liturgy:

> Good liturgy always says more than you mean; that is what makes it good. A liturgy that expressed no more than our mundane and limited hopes and fears would be so bad as to be unusable. The trouble with liturgy is not that it says too much, but that we may not notice that it is doing so.

Alongside this public liturgy, there continues the stream of private prayer. Many Christians have also heard and responded to the call to a more contemplative style of prayer in which the mystical element plays a stronger part. Evelyn Underhill, widely acknowledged to be one of this century's leading experts on mysticism, wrote a study on the nature and development of human spiritual consciousness in which she defines mysticism broadly as:

> the experience of the innate tendency of the human spirit towards complete harmony with the transcendental order; whatever be the theological formula under which that order is understood. This tendency, in great mystics, gradually captures the whole field of consciousness; it dominates their life and, in the experience called "mystic union", attains its end.[2]

Since those words were written in 1911, there have been many advances in our understanding of the working of the human psyche, though I was intrigued a little while ago to be present at a lecture in which one of our most celebrated experts on the working of the human brain frankly admitted that we know very little about it. What we do know is that it is possible for what seem to be mystical experiences to be in fact psychic phenomena akin to clairvoyance. One essential ingredient of the contemplative approach to God is the use of the imagination in such a way that it manages to escape from the earthbound realities which usually keep it tethered firmly to the ground, rather like a wartime barrage balloon which can rise to the end of its mooring but is thereafter incapable of further ascent. In the case of the mystic, the chain is severed and the imagination soars to heights of understanding normally unattainable, often returning to earth in due course with fresh insights into the knowledge of God.

It is difficult to make a hard and fast distinction between meditation and contemplation, though it is customary to confine the
former to what is called 'discursive' prayer (i.e. prayer that takes
the form of an internal discourse, a running to and fro) and the
latter to non-discursive prayer; however, the verbal distinction is
not all that important to the person who practises it. Behind it all
lies the attempt to know God, not so much through the processes
of the mind, though these are inevitably involved in all that we do,
but rather through the heart, seeking to know God through one's
capacity to love rather than solely through one's intellectual
capacity.

★   ★   ★

Prayer and art are natural companions, and for many artists their
work is a kind of prayer. This is particularly true of one special
form of Christian art, the icon, which is usually a painting on
wood of one of the saints of the Church, or of Jesus himself. Icons
are specially favoured, even venerated, in the Orthodox churches
of the east and are often of superlative aesthetic quality. With other
forms of art, too, the prayer can also be in the mind of the viewer
as well as in that of the artist. But if any work of art fails to draw a
positive spiritual response, the fault does not necessarily lie with
the artist: it could equally be the lack of aesthetic understanding in
the person who looks at it.

When a new work of art is being commissioned or sanctioned
for use in a church or cathedral, the relevant authorities will need
to assure themselves that it will do more than merely fill an empty
space. Does it stand in a proper relationship to its immediate
surroundings and to any other adjacent artistic work? Is it aesthetically good? Will it lead the worshippers in that place to pray and
to experience a genuine spiritual vision? In other words, will it
help to put people in touch with the living God whom they have
come to encounter in the liturgy, a liturgy to which art is closely
related?

Christian artists, as they set about their work, will no doubt
wish to do it within the context of lives in which prayer has a
significant role. By placing the whole creative process in the hands
of God, they are freeing their own hands to be the instrument
through which God can speak; by forgetting themselves, they can

become truly immersed in their work and so will not constantly be under the pressure of having to strive to achieve.

★ ★ ★

Religious music, especially when used liturgically, is of immense importance in creating the right atmosphere for worship: bad music can kill it, as can good music badly performed. Peter Jeffery, in an article entitled 'Chant East and West: Towards a Renewal of the Tradition', refers to Pope Pius X's words of 1903 on the principles regulating all sacred music:

> As its principal duty is to clothe the liturgical text ... with suitable melody, we read, it must possess "on the highest level" the three qualities that typify the liturgy itself: (1) holiness, (2) "goodness of form" giving it the character of "true art", and (3) universality. It is because "these qualities are found in the highest degree in Gregorian chant", that it takes precedence over other kinds of music.[3]

Bearing in mind the date, and the high office held by the original speaker, one would not wish to argue for much change in such a definition, though it would be interesting to know what the Pope meant by 'holiness' in this context. Interestingly, too, there seems to be something of a contemporary revival of plainsong, at least judging by the number of recordings currently available.

In a different context, St Augustine says that when you sing you are praying twice, which makes it all the more important to get the singing right in the first place. Even if it is impossible to set out clearly what makes suitable church music, and allowing· for the intermarriage between 'sacred' and 'secular', one of the fruits of good composition will always be the appropriateness of the music within the context of its use. 'Does it feel right?' is the question which needs to be answered. For example, there is something totally appropriate in the style of Herbert Howells' '*Collegium Regale*' setting of the Magnificat for use during the Church of England's service of Evensong: its meditative modal start, its surprising harmonies, its variations in texture and rhythm, its restraint in holding back the lower parts until verse 6, its return at the end to the placidness of the beginning, and then the powerful *Gloria Patri* with its allargando *Amen*.

It is not only the words that communicate, but the music itself, which can have its own complete existence without any words at all. Anyone who has had to struggle with learning a foreign language will realise that no real progress is made until one has mastered at least the rudiments of the three basic ingredients: grammar, vocabulary and pronunciation. Once these are reasonably secure, you can go abroad with some degree of confidence that you will understand and be understood. So with music, our appreciation and understanding are greatly improved when we have come to terms with its peculiarities of grammar, vocabulary and pronunciation, because with this enhancement comes a heightening of our aesthetic sensitivity. This does not mean that no-one who is musically illiterate can hope to appreciate good music: what is does mean is that those who do have this understanding are likely to experience more deeply the beauty of what they hear. Conversely, of course, the more you know about music, the more critical you are likely to be when it falls short!

The biblical starting point for our understanding of the theological significance of music is to be found in the creation narrative in the first chapter of Genesis, where God sees everything that he made, 'and behold, it was very good' (Genesis 1.31). The Report of the Archbishops' Commission on Church Music recognises this fundamental truth:

> No less than the earth and its resources, music is an integral part of God's great act of creation. Like all manifestations of truth, beauty, goodness and love in their many forms it has its origin in God. With its place in his design, it has a purpose.

> At the simplest level that purpose may be described as communication. In this music is not alone. Writing, painting and sculpture also communicate, as do speech, gesture and other means of expression which depend upon neither sound nor sight. Each has its place and each its distinctive way of conveying thoughts, ideas and emotions. But music, which is our concern here, is one of the most accessible and universal languages, being less limited than speech by social, intellectual, national or religious boundaries. It expresses, often more effectively than words, our feelings and aspirations. It is therefore widely employed in religious rituals, not only to address God but also to express his reality for the worshippers.[4]

The Report then goes on to describe how music is a revelation of God himself, its Creator, in 'his majesty and his simplicity, his righteousness and his mercy, his power and his gentleness, his mystery and his love'. The Church has a responsibility to encourage the development of musical and other artistic gifts as a result of its own concern for the redemption of the whole human person.

As far as the use of music in public worship is concerned, there will always be a degree of uncertainty or unpredictability about the effect of it on the individual, since so much depends not only on the way in which the worship is offered but also on the subjective psychological and spiritual states of the worshippers. Although in the end, only God is able to determine how good our worship has been aesthetically, there is still a weighty responsibility imposed on those who compose, select and perform it: of course we cannot avoid being subjective, but we can also use to the full such critical faculties as we may possess.

I have touched elsewhere on the problems encountered when we try to reconcile unacceptably low standards with good intentions. The Report takes up this theme, too, and offers this trenchant comment:

> Because perfection is unattainable here on earth, there is bound to be some falling short of the ideal. Worshippers readily forgive minor blemishes, but this should not be made an excuse for shoddy performances. Nor is there any justification for a popular notion that the standard of performance does not matter as long as it is sincere. It is not sincerity before God on the part of the musicians if they ignore the right notes or do not attempt to fulfil the intentions of the composer. After all, the skills of performers and composer alike are God-given and it is no glory to him to be musically careless. God may not be glorified by a congregation which has been set on edge by a needlessly low standard of singing or playing.[5]

During the five decades in which I have been involved in church music, as chorister, choirman, organist, choirmaster and clergyman, I have had ample opportunity to reflect on what it has meant to me, though I readily acknowledge that much has been happening at those deeper levels of which my conscious mind is not aware. There has been throughout a sense that this, for me, is the non-verbal medium above all others in which I am able to communicate with God, however haltingly as both speaker and listener. In music, whether I perform it or listen to it, I can go well beyond the spoken word and allow it to articulate that for which I have no speech, that which takes over *when words fail*.

I have found this to be true for me in a wide variety of musical forms such as hymns and anthems, organ and orchestral music, plainsong and polyphony. Nowhere, though, do I feel more lifted up in prayer and in tune with heaven than when listening to the Psalms, sung with poise and expression to Anglican chants, old and new. This is a profoundly satisfying aesthetic and spiritual experience which will assuredly strike chords with those who have a similar background of years of exposure to this particular form of music. To those who lack it, I can but apologise for speaking in what must seem like hyperbolic riddles, though I hope that they will warm to my understanding that worship can be a form of reality which we cannot generally experience in the other contexts of life.

> Public worship, in fact, has repercussions in the human soul. The experience, faith and thanksgiving which are the bone and sinew of worship are given back, as it were, revitalised at a higher voltage. Worship thus becomes not only the natural reaction to the experience of God's love but an important factor in the psychological and spiritual development of the worshipper. That development becomes more real as the worship is more real: the worship is more real as the attention of the whole man – body, emotions, mind, imagination – is centred on the idea of God.[6]

★   ★   ★

To do justice to the aesthetic links between prayer and literature would require several volumes the size of this one. Merely to try to explain the psychological processes which transport a Dante or a Blake from one mode of being into another, where even imagination seems to be transcended, would be a formidable, perhaps impossible, task. It is probably more helpful to concentrate very briefly on one of those pieces of contemporary literature that has already woven a thread in and out of these pages, namely the *Four Quartets* of T. S. Eliot.

This poem, or group of poems, is a piece of Christian spiritual writing almost without parallel this century, even though the name of Christ does not appear anywhere within it. But it is densely packed with references to scripture, to the Book of Common Prayer, and to a rich assortment of Christian mystics, such as our own indigenous Julian of Norwich and the unknown author of *The Cloud of Unknowing*. Unlike Eliot's much more obviously devotional work, *Ash Wednesday*, the *Four Quartets* are full more of tantalising allusions than of prayers openly expressed, but the underlying preoccupation with the nature of time allows him to drift very easily from time into eternity, and back again.

As in the devotional life of the Christian, there is no fixed style from start to finish but rather a series of contrasts in which different moods are expressed by different images and verbal constructs. The whole work repays careful reading, not just as a piece of twentieth-century 'Eng. Lit.' to be read in the classroom or the easy chair, but as a devotional work, taken slowly and prayerfully and allowing the vivid images to speak to us of the nature of time and life, of death and eternity.

> There are moments in which past and present and future are comprehended and relate us to the still point, which is also a point of view that interprets all of existence. In such moments we glimpse eternity – the reconciliation of opposites, real and ideal. Such moments find meaning only in memory, which unites past and future, so that passing moments in time can be contemplated in their eternity.[7]

The very first paradoxical words of the first poem, *Burnt Norton*, set out the agenda:

> Time present and time past
> Are both perhaps present in time future
> And time future contained in time past.

From there we pass on through that memorable line, 'At the still point of the turning world ... where past and future are gathered' to the total quietness which lies deep within us:

> Descend lower, descend only
> Into the the world of perpetual solitude,
> World not world, but that which is not world,
> Internal darkness, deprivation

> And destitution of all property,
> Dessication of the world of sense,
> Evacuation of the world of fancy,
> Inoperancy of the world of spirit.

East Coker has a similar paradoxical start with the words, 'In my beginning is my end'. Later we learn that

> The only wisdom we can hope to acquire
> Is the wisdom of humility: humility is endless.

Then, near the end of the poem, there comes the revelation:

> Love is most nearly itself
> When here and now cease to matter.

When Eliot writes in the third poem, *The Dry Salvages*, that 'We had the experience but missed the meaning', he is actually adumbrating, though in another context, a truth of the spiritual life: so often do we fail to perceive what lies behind the events which comes to us in daily life and to grasp the reality which is 'Emmanuel', God with us.

'To apprehend the point of intersection of the timeless with time, is an occupation for the saint', we are told, but for the more ordinary people, such as most of us are, there are only

> Hints followed by guesses; and the rest
> Is prayer, observance, discipline, thought and action.

The hint half-guessed, the gift half-understood, is Incarnation:

> Here the impossible union
> Of spheres of existence is actual,
> Here the past and future
> Are conquered, and reconciled.

The final poem, *Little Gidding*, takes us back to seventeenth-century Huntingdonshire and to the experiment of religious community life under Nicholas Ferrar. The times and seasons are again explored and probably the best-known lines of all Eliot's poetry appear:

104

If you came this way,
Taking any route, starting from anywhere,
At any time or at any season,
It would always be the same: you would have to put off
Sense and notion. You are not hear to verify,
Instruct yourself, or inform curiosity
Or carry report. You are here to kneel
Where prayer has been valid. And prayer is more
Than an order of words, the conscious occupation
Of the praying mind, or the sound of the voice praying.

This is the most explicitly Christian part of the *Four Quartets* and
is filled with powerful and prayerful images, allusions and quotations, its closing words containing a direct quotation from *The
Revelations of Divine Love* by the fourteenth-century English
mystic, Julian of Norwich:

Quick now, here, now, always-
A condition of complete simplicity
(Costing not less than everything)
And all shall be well and
All manner of things shall be well
When the tongues of flames are in-folded
Into the crowned knot of fire
And the fire and the rose are one.

As with so much of our praying, it is not always the words themselves that carry the prayer upwards like the smoke of incense, so
much as the images that lie behind and beyond the words, because
there does come a point in prayer *when words fail*. Ultimately, we
may find ourselves left with but one word, the word 'God', the
word that stands for liberty and integrity:

In praying, nothing matters so much as the name of God – "I am
who I am – I am with you" – that name which points to the utterly
free by refusing an ordinary name which would limit it, and yet
promotes a continual and unbreakable relationship.[8]

10 *Proclamation*

A centre of healing, teaching and medical research may not seem to be the most likely place to find one of the twentieth-century's outstanding pieces of art: yet, because of its squarish shape, wherever you sit in the synagogue at the Hadassah-Hebrew University Medical Centre in Kiryat Hadassah, Jerusalem, you find yourself looking up at three of a set of twelve windows by the Russian Jewish artist, Marc Chagall. The best way to appreciate them is to move slowly round the four points of the compass so that you view each set head on. Each window is impressive in its own right: collectively, they are extremely powerful, even overwhelming, and it is as a collection that they should be viewed.

The artist himself has described his work as 'my modest gift to the Jewish people, who have always dreamt of biblical love, of friendship and peace among all people'. The project took two years to complete and can only be understood in the light of Chagall's deep sense of identification with the history of the Jewish people. Its inspiration is mainly biblical and it is a representation of the twelve sons of the Patriarch Jacob and the blessings they received, expressed in a richness of symbolism which matches the richness of the colours used in their creation.

A few years ago, an article in *Theology* bore the intriguing title, 'Homage to Chagall the Theologian'. We are certainly right to think of him as one of the outstanding artists of our day but the word 'theologian' is not one that would as readily leap into our minds. As the writer points out:

> In one sense it is absurd to speak of an artist as being a theologian. He is a creator of things, not a philosophizer about God. Yet ... the great artist is inevitably a prophet – a product of his culture and a commentator on it.[1]

The same observation could be fittingly applied to several other modern artists. Some have used their chosen medium as a way of proclaiming what they believe to be the truth about God and about God's dealings with humankind; for others, the proclamation has been a by-product of what they were attempting to do. It is simply not true that contemporary artists have turned their backs on the great themes of religion. No one who has seen Norman Blamey's very realistic religious paintings and portraits of the Church of England in action could possibly doubt this.

The possibility of there being a proclamation of God in our creative works forms the core of this chapter and will be illustrated particularly through painting, music and poetry. These are far from being the only media for the telling forth of the glory of God as perceived by the human eye and ear, but are three of the most powerful ways through which something of the greatness and glory of God is revealed at that point *when words fail*. This is because each depends on the appropriate use of symbol and imagery, rather than on the use of prose, as the primary means of communication.

Liturgy, through which the people of God express their corporate worship of the Most High, combines many different aesthetic and theological elements, such as architecture, poetry, literature, music, colour and light. Its language is of the utmost importance in achieving the right end, as Cranmer and others before and since have clearly recognised. Words are splendid vehicles for the communication of ideas and emotions and, when rightly used, they are an indispensible component of our common prayer. They also have two great drawbacks: words can fossilize the truths they are attempting to convey, by so hemming them in that their essential content becomes incapable of further expression; and they can themselves become fossilized as language changes over the years and centuries, so giving the impression that there is something essentially antique or archaic about church services, which divorces them from the reality of contemporary life.

One wonders what Cranmer's reaction would be to the discovery that the words of the first English Prayer Book of 1549 are still recognisably in use four and a half centuries later. He might be agreeably flattered that the music of his own words continues to transport people, but it certainly runs counter to his underlying philosophy that the language of worship should be the best that is currently available, a language readily 'understood by the people'.

★   ★   ★

Those who have no expertise in any artistic field are often confused as to the criteria by which some work of art is to be judged. Can we rely simply on the wholly subjective view that if we like a piece of music, a painting or a poem, then that music, that painting or that poem is good and beautiful? There are clearly some problems with such an approach, but equally there are difficulties in leaving the judgement to those 'experts' who can come up with a set of objective criteria which will guarantee that what we see or hear is, or is not, good and beautiful. The appalling piece of mid-Victorian stained glass, universally condemned by all who know about such things and who possess an adequate scale of comparison, is the very thing which a visitor to a church will seize on and say, 'Isn't it lovely?' The miserable and mawkish hymn tune, with its saccharine harmonies, is the one which the worshippers actually enjoy singing, as opposed to the fine, strong and simple 16th-century tune. Who are we to set ourselves up as judges in these matters?

Yet there must be more to art than merely what I see or hear in it, otherwise we have a situation which is so totally anarchic that it can never mirror the order and purpose of a God who, in his creation, has shown himself to be orderly and purposeful.

> It is obvious that people often disagree about what they find beautiful but the very fact that where such disagreements occur we can talk, put forward reasons for our judgements, be understood and perhaps modify our views somewhat, indicates some shared criteria of judgement.[2]

This is why it is important for us to form our own judgements as to what is beautiful, but to do it from an aesthetic data base which is as wide as possible, which is constantly being updated, and which takes due note of what is said by those who are experts in their particular field. Without this, our own proclamation of what is good and truthful and lovely will be immeasurably impoverished.

Strangely enough, artists are in a particular difficulty here, because they are working intuitively, and that makes any sort of analysis of their work anathema. As is sometimes said in other contexts, so it is specially true in this one, analysis can lead to paralysis.

For artists who are Christians, the proclamation of the Gospel is an essential part of their response to the encounter with God. For St Paul, it was a divine imperative that he should proclaim Christ, one in which he has no choice. Even though his standing as an Apostle entitles him to material rewards for his spiritual labours, he refuses to stand on his rights, simply because he can do no other:

> For necessity is laid upon me. Woe to me if I do not preach the gospel! For if I do this of my own will, I have a reward; but if not of my own will, I am entrusted with a commission. What then is my reward? Just this: that in my preaching I may make the gospel free of charge, not making full use of my right in the gospel. (1 Corinthians 9.16–18)

The manner of that proclamation will take many different forms. For one it will be the simple witness of a life lived close to God, a closeness perhaps largely hidden from the world but resulting in the unmistakable serenity which speaks of an essential inner goodness. For another it will involve a life of dedicated service to humanity, yet one which springs not merely from a humanitarian concern but from a compulsion to do for others what Christ has done for us. For one, the emphasis will be on the actual preaching of the Gospel, using that word 'preaching' as:

> the proclamation with authority of the Gospel of Jesus Christ ... to turn people towards him by deepening their knowledge of him and their commitment to him.[3]

For another, the proclamation will be expressed in, for example, painting or music, through which the presence and the reality of God will be made visible or audible, not to titillate the emotions but to convey through sound or colour that in Christ nothing is ever the same again.

A true encounter with God is the key to a life which thereafter concentrates its energies on 'mission', on being sent back from the presence of God into the world, deriving its inspiration from the vision of God which it has received, dim or uncertain as that vision may be.

$\star \quad \star \quad \star$

One of the questions most frequently asked by those who have any interest in the relationship between theology and aesthetics is, 'Can there be any such thing as Christian art?' The answer, I believe, has to be that there is, and not solely when a particular painting happens to be of a religious subject. Paradoxically, a picture of, say, a steel foundry at work might be more Christian than one of the Adoration of the Magi, not because of the subject but because of the spirit in which the work was undertaken and the spiritual convictions of the artist.

The theologian will properly remind us that Christianity is an incarnational religion, that God became man in Jesus Christ, in order to reveal himself more fully to the world. 'No one has ever seen God', the author of the Fourth Gospel tells us in the last verse of his Prologue, but 'the only Son, who is in the bosom of the Father, he has made him known' (St John 1.18). It is therefore a very godly thing for artists to bring before our eyes manifestations of the unseen God, even though they may have little or no awareness that this is happening. Here we enter again the realm of signs and symbols and icons:

> Works of art are often described, rather loosely in many cases, as being symbolic. This means that they are more than just a sign, which points towards something, but in some interior way are participating in that to which they refer. A symbolic image is one with associations, bringing out a superior reality; a sign but far more than a sign. In fact a work of art that is symbolic is one that can stand by itself and also participate in something beyond itself.[4]

Those words of Michael Day touch on the sacramental, almost priestly, role of the artist's work, which is to reflect how things truly are in the eternal world, and thus to serve also in a prophetic capacity. Old Testament characters such as Amos, Hosea and Micah are 'prophets' not because they have a gift of looking at the future and surprising their contemporaries with forecasts of things to come. Their prophetic ability lies rather in their foretelling of the impending judgement of God, who is both just and loving, on those who persistently ignore his laws and flout his will.

In every generation there have been artists who recall the people to those values which are true, honourable, pure, lovely and gracious, to echo the words of Saint Paul (Philippians 4.8).

They condemn things that are meretricious; they sound a note of protest against what is bogus and sham; they strip off the veneers of artificiality; they allow the symbols to speak clearly of those truths which they represent.

*   *   *

The enormous quantity of painting of biblical themes is a reminder that artists in every generation have attempted to express their own faith through their particular medium. It may be that the response they now evoke is a good deal more muted than it was in previous ages, as an inevitable result of a gradual decline of popular Christianity, yet it would never have occured to our medieval ancestors (whether sculptors or painters) that what they were doing was in any sense separable from their everyday lives and from the faith which was part and parcel of them.

'Art' was not a 'subject' which required a special title. What they wanted to do was to tell the story of the mighty acts of God in a way which made them accessible to those who were unable to read, even were they to have had access to the written word.

> So the story of Jesus was told in sermons. Soon artists told it in paintings and sculpture. Musicians recounted it in song. Weavers used it as the theme for tapestry. Metalworkers took events from the story for their casting. Poets told it in meter. Glaziers fashioned brilliant windows to reflect the events and symbols found in the story. Translators made the story available in hundreds of languages. Wealthy patrons commissioned artists to use their genius to adorn churches, palaces and homes with pictures of events from the life of Jesus.[5]

From time to time a new development would take place under the influence of some parallel development in theological thought. Giotto, for example, in the early fourteenth-century, brought into the world of painting a new understanding of the significance of the individual, as a result of the renewed emphasis on the 'nobility of the individual'[6], which came through the influence of St Francis of Assisi. A century later, Fra Angelico (himself a friar, though in this case a Dominican) allows his work to speak of his own 'fundamental simplicity and devotion to God'.

Art critics have observed an evolution over the centuries in which successive schools of artists have portrayed their religious themes in gradually changing styles. It has become necessary, as we have seen, to recoin an ancient term, 'aesthetics', in order to approach works of art in general from a particular viewpoint.

However, one's perception of aesthetic values depends quite considerably on the standpoint from which they are approached. Jacques Maquet, in a book subtitled, 'An Anthropologist Looks at the Visual Arts', illustrates these different emphases:

> Art has been mainly "built" by art historians as a fairly autonomous domain in which chronology and the sequence of schools and styles are the main issues. For some philosophers, art is a contingent manifestation of a transcendental beauty. For art critics, the visual objects express the intentions and skills of an individual artist. For experimental psychologists, art is a stimulus generating response whose variations may be measured. Psychiatrists see in art a sublimation of repressed impulses, and art dealers see a source of market commodities.[7]

The same author adds that the actual aesthetic experience results from 'an encounter between a subject, the beholder, and an object whose forms are aesthetically significant'. When this is translated into the meeting between a viewer and a work of art which is clearly of a 'religious' nature, it is irrelevant that the work itself may happen to be of a subject that many would consider uninteresting or even repellent. The practical effect of this is sometimes very confusing for the viewer, who finds it difficult to come to a decision about the work because there is a struggle going on in the mind between the evaluation of the skill of the artist in portraying the object as a work of art, and the need to balance this by the realisation that the object itself may be inherently unattractive. There is, therefore, a dichotomy between the nature of the object and the manner of its proclamation.

Few people are not capable of making art, even those of us who did it so badly that we were thrown out of the art class at school. The child is capable of making an artistic declaration which, in its honesty, may be superior to that of the trained artist. One inherent danger in all art education is that artists can be taught a technique which deprives both them and the viewer of truth. Sometimes the pendulum swings too far in the opposite direction, when technical training of any kind is perceived to be an inhibiting factor. Life would be much easier for the artist, and for the rest of us, if there were certain aesthetic golden rules: it would also, no doubt, be very much less exciting.

For a piece of art to be a proclamation, it may be decorative, celebratory or educative, or a combination of any or all of these three factors. We know from our own experience how significant is the impact of colour upon us: look round any shop, school, factory, office, home or hospital to see the truth of this. Even something which is intended to be 'purely' decorative makes an important statement about itself as well as revealing something of the artist's intention. In its celebratory aspect, art relies heavily on colour, proclaiming (for example) a major Christian festival brightly and boldly. This happens to be particularly true for Islam, where figurative art is prohibited, and less so, though for the same reason, in Judaism, where much of its artistic talent has found freedom of expression more in music and poetry. In its educative role, art records not merely an event, but the significance of the event, be it religious or political, through such media as wallpaintings and tapestries. We have also become familiar in recent decades with the work of the 'official artist', who records the progress of a war or of a judicial trial.

In the end, the artist is really trying to proclaim what he has discovered through his exploration of the spirit of nature, or of man, or of God, by presenting to those who will look at it the presence and reality of life. What makes the artist different from the rest of us is not a particular talent for drawing or painting so much as the ability to look intently at something – a flower or a wave breaking – with no preconceived ideas whatsoever, and to bring that flower or wave into the present: it is this 'making real' which is the most important part of the whole activity.

* * *

Music, even more than painting, has for hundreds of years been used consciously as a way of proclaiming God through creative work. Like painting, sculpture and architecture, it relies largely on a language which is intrinsically non-verbal. It has a vocabulary which is peculiar to itself and a natural suitability for use in worship, though as Donald Whittle has pointed out:

It was not until Augustine's *De Musica* that an adequate critique of music and theology was put forward. In this work Augustine speaks of music as an activity of the reason, not merely a matter of feeling and self-expression, and that which is 'bad' in music he sees as part of the heritage of imperfection in all creation.[8]

There have always been those who have viewed the liturgical use of music with some degree of reservation, even suspicion. Might it not, they would argue, detract from, rather than enhance, the work with which it is associated, debase and cheapen rather than enrich and ennoble? Even among those who argue strongly for the inclusion of music in acts of worship, there are diverging views as to what is admissible and what should be rejected. We see but the latest manifestation of this debate when church musicians argue today the pros and cons of guitars and organs, of plainchant or Anglican chant. Some would argue that it matters little what you do so long as you do it to the glory of God. The temptation to go along with this attitude is readily apparent, since to run counter to it suggests not only musical snobbery but, far worse, that God is not concerned with our minds so long as our hearts are in the right place!

Whereas most church music is itself a vehicle for the proclamation of the Gospel, there is also plenty of other music which addresses the great themes of religion, from the creation of the universe to the final apocalypse. In doing so, it makes use of a variety of forms, including myth, legend, fable, fairy-tale and straightforward history. Writing on the first of these, myth, in an editorial entitled, 'Who's Afraid of Richard Wagner?', John Drury writes about the nineteenth-century German composer who, he says:

> provides a colossal corrective to the widespread view that 'myth' means flimsy nonsense. In the *Ring* cycle he left a vast story of the beginning and end of the human world, its fall and redemption, which, like the biblical version, drew on various sources to produce a work whose evocative power is an index of the significant power of myth.[9]

Whatever the musician's chosen form may be, we cannot always assume that a piece of music which is not associated with a religious theme cannot therefore be good 'religious' music, any more than we can assume that a musical work which is illustrative of a biblical subject must always and inevitably be good religious music. One tantalising question, which we may seldom be able to answer, because it is such a difficult thing to pin down, is to ask ourselves what was the composer's intention? Was it to fulfil a commission to write an oratorio that led to a hasty work, ill-thought-out and full of the worst kind of musical clichés, or was it to express something which seemed to come overwhelmingly from outside the composer's own experience, almost as if he had been taken over by some power beyond himself?

The Christian Church has since its earliest days used music as one of the ways through which the believing community strives to express a sense of the lifting up of the soul to God and, wherever possible, to do it as beautifully as may be, both in its composition and in its performance. It has been observed of music that:

> "being (unlike architecture) un-material, (unlike painting) uncon-cerned with representation of physical objects, and (unlike poetry) independent of ideas, it is able to fly, unburdened, into regions beyond their utmost reach." [10]

Although this statement is somewhat misleading (for example, much 'programme' music does represent physical objects, and 'ideas' need not only be verbal ones), it serves to remind us that music has the capacity to take us into realms which architecture, painting and poetry cannot reach.

No one who has the responsibility for ordering public worship can long remain unaware of the problems surrounding the choice of music which reflects what would generally be considered 'good taste', music which may well be deceptively simple but which also possesses real quality. We have already observed how members of a congregation will reject a good new hymn tune in favour of the dull one on which it has been brought up. How rewarding it is to find them actually enjoying the new one (perhaps after a congre-gational music practice) when they have discovered its real quality. In the end, it all resolves itself into finding the right answer to the question, 'How can God best be proclaimed through the medium of music?' Perhaps it is just as well that there is no one, simple, straightforward and infallible answer to that question.

★   ★   ★

The other major area of aesthetics which deserves to be looked at in terms of 'proclamation' is poetry. Aware as I am that there is much religious poetry which is not written from within the Christian tradition or about that tradition, I will for the sake of brevity limit this consideration to that tradition, though it must again be with the caveat that not all overtly Christian poetry is good religious poetry, any more than all non-Christian poetry is not religious.

Consider the words of that greatest of all modern theologians writing on aesthetic matters, Hans Urs von Balthasar:

> Christianity is really "an inspiration" such as is expressed both in the ethical sphere (above all as love of one's neighbour) and in the aesthetic (as an exact experiencing of the forms of the world) with the most careful, most sober endeavour. It is precisely the duty of the one who ascends to Christ in faith, hope and love to interpret all the forms of God's revelation in Christ throughout the universe, and this task is achieved by Hopkins the poet. For what has to be interpreted is not concepts (of "universal", abstract truths) but images (of the unique, personal, divine-human truth), and here poetry is the absolutely appropriate theological language and Hopkins brings the great English tradition back into the Church by his own creative achievement.[11]

Let us, then linger for a while with **Gerard Manley Hopkins** (1844–1889) and note some of those 'images of the unique divine-human truth' as expressed by this artistic master craftsman, close friend of Robert Bridges and, for the last twelve years of his short life, a Jesuit priest. In his major work, *The Wreck of the Deutschland*, written in memory of five Franciscan nuns who were drowned in 1875, we find lines such as these:

> I kiss my hand
> To the stars, lovely-asunder
> Starlight, wafting him out of it; and
> Glow, glory in thunder;
> Kiss my hand to the dappled-with-damson west;
> Since, tho' he is under the world's splendour and wonder,
> His mystery must be instressed, stressed;
> For I greet him the days I meet him, and bless when I
> understand. [12] [v.5]

It dates from day
Of his going in Galilee;
Warm-laid grave of a womb-life grey;
Manger, maiden's knee;
The dense and the driven Passion, and frightful sweat. [12] [v.7]

Joy fall to thee, father Francis,
Drawn to the Life that died;
With the gnarls of the nails in thee, niche of the lance, his
Lovescape crucified
And seal of his seraph-arrival! and these thy daughters
And fire-lived and leaved favour and pride,
Are sisterly sealed in wild waters,
To bathe in his fall-gold mercies, to breathe in his all-fire
    glances. [12] [v.23]

The whole poem is indeed alive with this kind of inventive imagery and the reader will only obtain its full flavour by letting that imagery dwell in the mind, without attempting to dissect every line and every word. A much shorter poem, about the kestrel, is called *The Windhover* and is headed, 'To Christ our Lord'. With its alliteration, its allusion to the crucifixion, its tremendous sense of movement, and its frequent use of hyphenated adjectives, this short poem is worth quoting in full as a fine example of Hopkins's unique skill:

I caught this morning morning's minion, kingdom of
    daylight's dauphin, dapple-dawn-drawn Falcon, in
    his riding
Of the rolling level underneath him steady air and striding
High there, how he rung upon the rein of a wimpling wing
In his ecstasy! then off, off forth on swing,
As a skate's heel sweeps smooth on a bow-bend:
    the hurl and gliding
Rebuffed the big wind. My heart in hiding
Stirred for a bird, – the achieve of, the mastery of the thing!

Brute beauty and valour and act, oh, air, pride, plume, here
Buckle! AND the fire that breaks from thee then, a billion
Times told lovelier, more dangerous. O my chevalier!

No wonder of it: sheer plod makes plough down sillion
Shine, and blue-bleak embers, ah my dear,
Fall, gall themselves, and gash gold vermillion. [13]

Equally fine effects are to be found in *God's Grandeur*, *The Blessed Virgin Compared to the Air We Breathe* and *Pied Beauty*, among others.

Nearer to the present day is the former Poet Laureate, **Sir John Betjeman** (1906–1984). His *Church Poems* savour the unmistakable sights, sounds and smells of English churches, with their constant references to tall towers, swinging bells and decaying mustiness. This extract from one of his most familiar works catches both the commitment and the artistry:

> And is it true? And is it true,
> This most tremendous tale of all,
> Seen in a stained-glass window's hue,
> A Baby in an ox's stall?
> The maker of the stars and sea
> Become a Child on earth for me?
>
> And is it true? For if it is,
> No loving fingers tying strings
> Around those tissued fripperies,
> The sweet and silly Christmas things,
> Bath salts and inexpensive scent
> And hideous tie so kindly meant,
>
> No love that in a family dwells,
> No carolling in frosty air,
> Nor all the steeple-shaking bells
> Can with this single Truth compare-
> That God was Man in Palestine
> And lives today in Bread and Wine.[14]

Certainly the thought lacks the profundity of Hopkins and yet the proclamation of the faith is loud, clear, simple and, above all, accessible in this poem which he simply calls 'Christmas'.

The Welsh priest, **R. S. Thomas**, has produced some of the finest poetry written in the English language during this century. One example from the considerable corpus must suffice: it is called 'Directions':

> In this desert of language
>   we find ourselves in,
> with the sign-post with the word "God"
>   worn away
>   and the distance ...?

Pity the simpleton
  with his mouth open crying:
    How far is it to God?

And the wiseacre says: Where you were,
friend.
  You know that smile
    glossy
as the machine that thinks it has outpaced
  belief?
    I am one of those
who sees from the arms opened
  to embrace the future
the shadow of the Cross fall
  on the smoothest of surfaces
    causing me to stumble.[15]

There is a long tradition of Christian poetry from the anonymous medieval writers, through Chaucer and Spenser, Campion and Donne, Herrick and Milton, Crashaw and Baxter, Vaughan and Traherne, Watts and Wesley, Cowper and Keble, Patmore and Rosetti, Eliot and Bridges, to Kaan and Dudley-Smith. The quality, naturally enough, is variable but all have spoken to the depths of someone's soul, either in their own generation or subsequently. It is also worth recording that a great deal of what many Christians know about the faith has been communicated through poetry, with familiar hymns impressing their theology on the minds of those who sing them, week by week and season by season.

Whether we read his words as a poem, sing them as a hymn to Basil Harwood's tune 'Luckington', or listen to them as an anthem with music by Ralph Vaughan Williams, George Herbert calls for the praises of God to be proclaimed in earth and heaven, by the Church and by the individual soul:

Let all the world in every corner sing,
My God and King.
The heavens are not too high,
His praise may thither fly:
The earth is not too low,
His praises there may grow.
Let all the world in every corner sing,
My God and King.

Let all the world in every corner sing,
My God and King.
The Church with psalms must shout,
No door can keep them out;
But above all the heart
Must bear the longest part.
Let all the world in every corner sing,
My God and King.

★   ★   ★

Proclamation is achieved in a variety of ways and its importance for the Christian faith is vital. In an age with ever-increasing facilities for communication, particularly through the use of electronic means, we face the twofold risk either of allowing our aesthetic standards to fall below an acceptable level in our enthusiasm to seize every opportunity, or of setting such impossibly high targets that Christians are led to believe that those who are doing the proclaiming live in a world where the spiritual air is rarefied to such a degree that no real contact can be made with it. This is a dilemma which presents itself to every age: it does not excuse us from trying to achieve a satisfactory compromise.

11 *Passion*

The south garth of the twelfth-century Abbey Church of St Mary and St Ethelflaeda in Romsey, Hampshire, is a tranquil oasis separated from the busy streets of the town centre by no more than a row of shops with their small back gardens. There, on the west wall of the south transept, and seen at its best when lit by the descending summer sun, is the famous Romsey Rood. This figure of the crucified Christ, is very nearly a thousand years old:

> it shows Jesus as the Lord who reigns, with his arms outstretched, eyes open, and head held high, with the "hand of God" coming from a cloud above.[1]

There is a wonderful simplicity, yet also an immense strength, in this stone carving of 'the faithful witness, the first-born of the dead'. (Revelation 1.5) It goes right to the heart of the Christian faith, to the eternal mystery of the passion, crucifixion and resurrection of Jesus Christ.

No study of aesthetics can afford to neglect the powerful influence of suffering on the portrayal of the pilgrimage of mankind through the ages and it is in this sense of suffering that I use the word 'passion' in this chapter. Suffering has shaped the life of humanity, as well as having inspired it to rise to the highest of which it is capable. Suffering is an inescapable fact of life and, ultimately, a profound theological mystery, in which the presence of evil in the world has to be set against God's gift to mankind of freedom. The language of theodicy asks why a righteous God allows such appalling suffering in the world, often afflicting those who appear to be totally innocent and blameless. If he is almighty, why does he not use his power to bring suffering to an end? If he is really loving, why does he treat us so unjustly?

This is a serious problem for belief, though not within the scope of this book to explore in depth. A clue to the answer is to be found in the victory of Christ himself over suffering and death, together with our own faith in the good and loving purposes of God. Much of the truly great music, literature, painting and sculpture of the world is a reflection on this paradox, as writers and composers, artists and craftsmen have struggled to express both the reality of suffering and the conquest of it under the power of God.

The 'problem of evil' long predates the Christian revelation: theologians and philosophers have been exploring it ever since people began to contemplate the nature of their existence in the world. Most of the major religions have attempted to present some kind of solution to the problem. Within the Christian era, it has come to the fore as a matter of debate at various stages, particularly during the Patristic period; in the Middle Ages; at the 'Enlightenment' of the eighteenth-century; and again during the present century, which has seen so much suffering on such a wide scale, notably in two world wars, and most vividly in the Jewish Holocaust and in the devastation caused by the use of atomic weapons.

It is very difficult today to justify the view held by many people of different cultures and times that suffering is a form of divine punishment for erring mankind. Clearly there are kinds of suffering which bear a close or even direct relationship to various sins of excess, but the Christian theologian will find little evidence to make a specific cause-and-effect association between all sin and all suffering. It is equally clear that those who have themselves suffered bring a special quality of understanding, or empathy, to those who are currently undergoing it, thus suffering is not entirely negative in its results. Indeed, it is often through suffering that we grow in moral stature as disciples of Jesus Christ, who in his own person fulfils the prophecies of Isaiah concerning the 'Suffering Servant':

> He was despised and rejected by men; a man of sorrows, and acquainted with grief; and as one from whom men hide their faces he was despised, and we esteemed him not. Surely he has borne our griefs and carried our sorrows; yet we esteemed him stricken, smitten by God, and afflicted. But he was wounded for our transgressions, he was bruised for our iniquities; upon him was the chastisement that made us whole, and with his stripes we are healed. (Isaiah 53.3–5)

No one has ever succeeded in giving a wholly satisfying answer to the problem of evil in a world created by a good God. It is little consolation to the father whose two year old son dies of leukaemia that this very experience may one day enable him to help someone in a similar position. It is not much use to tell a woman whose husband is the latest victim of a series of sectarian murders in Northern Ireland that the grief she must now go through will somehow or other strengthen her character in the future, true as that may well be. What we can do, though, is to point again and again to the victory of Christ over evil, pain and death, and to his promise that he is with us in our own sufferings. The Christian is not to deny the existence of evil, nor remain unconcerned at it or detached from it, but rather to accept the reality of it, to wage war against it and to hold to the certainty that good triumphs in the end.

One of the most sensitive studies of this whole problem is to be found in John Hick's book, *Evil and the God of Love*, from which the following lines are taken:

> At the outset of an attempt to present a Christian theodicy – a defence of the goodness of God in face of the evil in His world – we should recognize that, whether or not we can succeed in formulating its basis, an implicit theodicy is at work in the Bible, at least in the sense of an effective reconciliation of profound faith in God with a deep involvement in the realities of sin and suffering. The Scriptures reflect the characteristic mixture of good and evil in human experience ... Even the greatest evil of all, the murder of the son of God, has been found by subsequent Christian faith to be also, in an astounding paradox, the greatest good of all.[2]

This 'greatest good of all' has been one of the most powerful influences on the arts that the world has ever known. The crucifixion itself has been, and still is today, a potent symbol and image of a power which would be ineffectual without the suffering which is an integral part of it. The depiction of the Passion is repeated in some form or other in thousands of churches and cathedrals throughout the world. Sometimes the image of the Crucified is as one might have seen it on Calvary: stark, agonised. Sometimes it is the figure of a robed and crowned monarch, reigning from the tree of glory. In one church, the cross towers above the screen or below the chancel arch; in another, it will be placed on or behind the altar. In one, the image will be of stone, in another of wood, or metal, or fibreglass. Some emphasize the desolation, the emptiness and the seeming defeat of Good Friday; others stress God's victory over evil, the triumph of Christ over darkness and death.

★   ★   ★

St Francis of Assisi has been a rich source of inspiration to artists ever since the thirteenth-century, including such great masters as Cimabue and Giotto. It was in the year 1206, on a day when he was meditating on a crucifix in the ruined church of San Damiano that he heard the call of Christ to 'Go and restore my house'. The twofold consequence of this divine command was first the actual restoration of that particular building, and then the dedication of his own life to restoring the Church of Christ during the twenty years that remained to him.

St Francis was neither the first nor the last disciple of the crucified Jesus to be moved by his contemplation of the cross of Christ and to see beyond the tragedy, the pain and the death to the glory, the liberation and the life. Those who today seek to understand the mystery of the atonement need to remember that the crucifixion is incomprehensible not only without the resurrection, but also without the life which preceded it.

That life was a human life: divine, but fully human, too, and it is the life which we all share by virtue of our own humanity. It is from within their own experience of that humanity that artists and sculptors, poets and novelists, architects and musicians have attempted to interpret the mystery of suffering, frequently from first-hand experience of pain, grief, loneliness, poverty, bereavement, physical handicap and anxiety. The paradoxical words of St Paul, 'When I am weak, then I am strong' (2 Corinthians 12.10b) were not the product of a theologian sitting down at his desk and deliberately producing a statement calculated to confuse simple believers. It was the utterance of a man who had endured just about every imaginable kind of suffering because of his belief in Christ. In the context of what he calls 'boastful confidence' in God, he sets out some of the things he had experienced as an apostle:

> Five times I have received at the hands of the Jews the forty lashes less one. Three times I have been beaten with rods; once I was stoned. Three times I have been shipwrecked; a night and a day I have been adrift at sea; on frequent journeys, in danger from rivers, danger from robbers, danger from my own people, danger from Gentiles, danger in the city, danger in the wilderness, danger at sea, danger from false brethren; in toil and hardship, through many a

sleepless night, in hunger and thirst, often without food, in cold and exposure. (2 Corinthians 11.24–27)

These are not the experiences of the majority of Christians today, though countless believers have suffered horribly in the persecutions of our own time, whether in Russia or China, Uganda or South Africa, Chile or Nicaragua. Yet there are many others, people whom we ourselves know, who can say that they came to a point in their lives where the pressures from outside or from within were well nigh unbearable. Many of these people have also made the incredible discovery that from what seems like a kind of death, there emerges a new life, a paradox which perhaps lies within our own first-hand experience. 'When I am weak, then I am strong' appears to be self-contradictory, but it is true. Solzhenitsyn's book, *Gulag Archipelago*, tells how time and time again, the men and women who passed through the appalling horrors of the penal system in post-Revolution Russia have been at their truly greatest when the material circumstances of their lives were unthinkably bad: the author himself produced some of his finest thoughts when the immediate outlook was bleak beyond words.

It may be a fact of life that no truly great artist in any field has reached the climax of his or her powers until some major catastrophe has had to be faced, such as bereavement, hunger or insanity. Therefore we need not be unduly surprised that Beethoven wrote some of his finest music after he became deaf, that Mozart composed much of his during illness, anxiety and poverty, and that Schubert wrote *Die Schöne Müllerin* when he was suffering intense physical pain as a patient in the Vienna General Hospital.

St Paul argued his case with God on more than one occasion: the answer he received was, 'My grace is sufficient for you, for my power is made perfect in weakness' (2 Corinthians 12.9). It was this divine grace that enabled him to cope not only with his 'thorn in the flesh' but also with weariness and slander, exhaustion and opposition. It was the same grace which seventeen centuries later enabled John Wesley to achieve an amazing daily average of three sermons and nearly sixty miles on horseback.

Some of Paul's sublimest thoughts, such as those contained in the Epistle to the Philippians, were written in a prison cell, as was John Bunyan's great work of literary and spiritual artistry, *The*

Pilgrim's Progress, as were some of the finest letters of the German anti-Nazi Lutheran pastor, Dietrich Bonhoeffer.

The greatest paradox of all is that God, though put to death, yet reigns from the Cross, where we see the Lord of life identified with death, the Light of the world enveloped in darkness, the water of life dying of thirst, and the lover of souls forsaken by men. Yet it is out of that suffering and pain and loneliness and misery, of which we all experience something in our lifetime, that new life comes.

Human suffering is set in the most understandable context if we remember that we are a pilgrim people: our journey takes us **through** this life but our true home lies **beyond** it, in heaven. C. S. Lewis has this to say in his book, *The Problem of Pain*:

> The Christian doctrine of suffering explains, I believe, a very curious fact about the world we live in. The settled happiness and security which we all desire, God withholds from us by the very nature of the world: but joy, pleasure, and merriment, He has scattered broadcast ... Our Father refreshes us on the journey with some pleasant inns, but will not encourage us to mistake them for home.[3]

★   ★   ★

Much church music is centred on the theme of suffering and in particular on the Passion of Christ. Until the seventeenth-century, the musical rendering of the Passion narrative was set to plainsong with choruses, and it is Heinrich Schütz who is usually credited with first having allocated the words of the various participants to individual soloists. Schütz (1585–1672) was building, however, on late medieval and Reformation sources, such as France's Gilles Binchois (1400–1460) and Germany's Johann Walther (1496–1570), who was the first to use his native language instead of the Church's language, Latin. The Schütz settings, though dependent on the Italian style which developed around Giovanni Gabrieli (1557–1612), and despite their occasional dramatic outbursts, impress the listener most strongly by their sense of austerity, an appropriate enough emotion for music which is reflecting the suffering of Christ.

His successors change the emphasis considerably, leading it away from the liturgical and towards the operatic, but it is J. S. Bach (1685–1750) who brings the genre to its apex with two of his greatest works, the *St Matthew Passion* (1729) and the (much shorter) *St John Passion* (1723). The former is universally regarded as the most outstanding of its kind, comparable with the B minor Mass, composed on the grand scale and notable for the wonderful harmonies of the various chorales, and for such imaginative touches as the use of a distinctive strings-only accompaniment for the dominical utterances and the great sense of controlled emotion in the shouts of the crowds.

As against the Puritan, who would prefer the words of the Gospel to speak for themselves, unadorned with music, the lover of beauty would contend that the significance and impact of works such as the *St Matthew Passion* are of the highest possible calibre. For those who have the ear to hear, they can enhance the original message of scripture and transport the mind and the soul of the listener into those higher realms where, even in this life, a foretaste of eternity is to be obtained.

These great works are not the sole possession of the Church and there is a sense in which they have come to be regarded as an integral part of the total musical heritage. In much the same way, there are countless works of classical music which have no specific religious associations but which are nevertheless capable of evoking a response which can safely be described as spiritual. One thinks, for example, of a Mozart opera, of Elgar's '*Enigma Variations*' or of Vaughan Williams's 'Pastoral' symphony.

The Requiem is another example of music which specifically reflects the theme of suffering, or passion. The Mass for the Dead, whilst omitting some of the more exuberant parts of the eucharistic liturgy, such as the 'Gloria in Excelsis', also contains a number of additions, chief among which is the medieval hymn, the 'Dies Irae' (the Day of Wrath). Ever popular among them are those by Mozart, Berlioz, Verdi and Brahms, though that of Brahms is not strictly a Requiem at all. Fauré's Requiem of 1887 has established for itself, and deservedly so, a phenomenal following during the past two or three decades, perhaps because it contains some memorable orchestral and vocal passages, such as the 'Pie Jesu' sung by a treble voice, and the introduction to the 'Agnus Dei', played on the strings. This, his only major sacred work, combines austerity with sensuality, and emphasises at the end the grace of God, who calls us, as he called Abraham, to be with him in the heavenly Jerusalem.

Standing as the sole representative of what is effectively a different literary genre is Edward Elgar's oratorio arrangement of John Henry Newman's poem, *The Dream of Gerontius*, composed for the Birmingham Musical Festival of 1890. The poem imagines what happens to the soul of a righteous man at, and immediately after, his death and contains words which have become even more famous in the form of the hymns, 'Praise to the Holiest in the height' and 'Firmly I believe and truly', though the tunes by Elgar are not those to which they are normally sung. Passion and anguish, loneliness and distress are all present in full measure, but so also are trust and hope, faith and serenity.

Another composition which illustrates the way in which a modern composer has written music to accompany words which tell of pain and death, is a contemporary 'passion', in which Christ suffers alongside the sufferings of humanity. Benjamin Britten (1913–1976) completed his *War Requiem* in 1961, the words being an amalgam of texts from the poems of Wilfred Owen and the Mass for the Dead. The 'Agnus Dei', for instance, begins with a tenor solo to the words:

> One ever hangs where shelled roads part.
> In this war He too lost a limb,
> But his disciples hide apart;
> And now the soldiers bear with Him.

The chorus then sings, extremely softly, the traditional Latin words of the 'Agnus Dei', with further verses of poetry interspersed. The overall effect is immensely moving as the twin sources interpret each other and are united into a harmonious unity.

*　　*　　*

We turn finally to literature, where once again we find a considerable output of writing which explores the 'passion' theme, a fact which need not surprise us when we reflect for a moment on our own experience of life, in which suffering sooner or later makes itself felt, sometimes to be ignored, sometimes to be escaped from, sometimes to be triumphed over. Few of the great novelists, dramatists and poets have not turned to it at some stage of their careers, often to treat it with such power that the result is itself illustrative of the ability of human nature to rise above even the worst that can be thrown at it.

Among the dramatists, **William Shakespeare** (1564–1610) is arguably the greatest exponent of this theme, with *King Lear* among his highest achievements. In *Macbeth, Hamlet, Othello, Julius Caesar*, and all the other tragedies, there are so many passages illustrative of his approach to suffering that it would be impossible to do justice to them in this work. One is left spellbound by the combination of profound experience and consummate skill which was able to turn out consistently the best of English poetry and drama in such enormous quantities.

Turning to the novelist, space permits us to select no more than a quartet, from the wealth of available material. Each is writing out of a different personal situation and each is addressing the theme of suffering in a different way. They all have the common denominator of having used their literary skills to create characters and situations which have a genuinely good aesthetic ring to them and which set off reverberations in the depth of our conscious or subconscious minds. In chronological order of their birth, they are Thomas Hardy, John Steinbeck, Graham Greene and William Golding. In choosing them, I am well aware that I am ignoring dozens of other novelists of many periods and nationalities: Dostoevsky, for example, from an earlier age and a different (Russian) culture, has much of very great importance and insight to say about suffering.

Thomas Hardy (1840–1928) began his career as an architect and was profoundly influenced by the life, and even more by the death by suicide, of Horace Moule. His first real literary success came with the publication in 1874 of *Far from the Madding Crowd* and this was followed in the next two decades by other major novels: *The Return of the Native* (1878), *The Trumpet Major* (1880), *The Mayor of Casterbridge* (1886), *Tess of the D'Urbervilles* (1891) and *Jude the Obscure* (1896). As well as this considerable output of long works, there was also a steady stream of short stories and poems. Writing mainly in Dorset and out of a deep knowledge and love of the Wessex countryside, he manages to convey the realities of life in all their richness, but not least those tragic elements which are so much a part of them.

This comes out very strongly, for example, in *Tess of the*

D'Urbervilles in which the eponymous heroine moves from one disaster to another, ending with her own execution for murder. The major characters of *Far from the Madding Crowd*, Bathsheba Everdene, Gabriel Oak, William Boldwood and Francis Troy all drink deeply from the cup of faithlessness, violence and madness in a story which moves inexorably along against a fine bucolic background, as if there were an inevitability about passion in God's 'plan'.

Other finely-drawn characters include Michael Henchard as *The Mayor of Casterbridge*, Jude Fawley and Sue Bridehead in *Jude the Obscure*, and Eustacia Vye and Damon Wildeve in *The Return of the Native*. Hardy's novels do not have the fairy-tale ending in which everyone lives happily together ever after: instead, they mirror their author's own acidity and disillusionment with contemporary church and community life. One recent commentator, in an article entitled 'Thomas Hardy's Flawed Universe', describes the writer's growing personal bitterness and religious antagonism:

> His distaste for the arrogance of nineteenth century clergy is not concealed. This dislike of the clergy was strengthened by the feeling of moral hypocrisy rife in nineteenth century society and often crystallised in the attitudes of the Church and given expression in the views and actions of the clergy.[4]

John Steinbeck (1902–1968) is a product of a different age and of a different culture: his background is twentieth century California rather than Victorian Dorset, yet his characters are drawn largely from the same stock of predominantly agricultural communities. The graphic portrayal of the interdependence of the itinerant farmhands, Lennie and George, the principal actors in *Of Mice and Men*, is a powerful reminder that everybody needs someone. The urban backcloth of *Cannery Row* proclaims a similar message through the inter-relationships of the residents of one particular street, all of whom share a common poverty. *Out of Eden* charts the vicissitudes of two American families and has been described as the chronicle of the nation's 'trek from East to West to discover an Eden that always somehow escapes us and that we as a people yet continue to hope for and believe in'.

It is generally accepted that Steinbeck's greatest work was *The*

Grapes of Wrath (1939), the tale of a community driven from its own soil in the dustbowl of Oklahoma, by the pressure of industrial progress, to look for a 'promised land' in the west, a promise which never actually materialises. Here again is life in all its richness, with the human spirit rising above everything that challenges it and the whole concept of passion or suffering addressed with profound sensitivity.

The novels of **Graham Greene** (1909–1991) bring us back to this country in the main, where the author was educated at Oxford, worked as a sub-editor on *The Times* and was received into the Roman Catholic Church in his mid-20s. The human predicament is examined from several different angles. Some of his books, including *The Confidential Agent* (1939), *The Third Man* (1950) and *Our Man in Havana* (1958) are set against a background of war and the consequences of war. Another group explores the concepts of good and evil, among them *Brighton Rock* (1938) with its seedy background of the criminal fraternity, *The Power and the Glory* (1940) which traces the life of a drunken priest at the time of the Mexican revolution, and *The Heart of the Matter* (1948) with the moral problems of a police chief in Africa as its central theme. Over a dozen other novels and various short stories tackle the concept of commitment, whether religious or political, and are set in such widely separated locations as Haiti, the Congo, Vietnam, Paraguay, Spain and England. As with Hardy and Steinbeck, again and again the reader is brought face to face with, and made to reflect on, pain and suffering, grief and death, which are integral to the reality of 'passion'.

A writer on the subject of 'Corruption and Grace in Graham Greene', notes that there is a lot more of the former than of the latter:

> The novelist harries a sad humanity to the limits of experience and beyond the limits of rational hope or confidence in a moral order. But beyond the limits, beyond the corruption of the world, there is room and opportunity for the grace of God.[5]

William Golding (1911–1993) writes from the dual background of teaching and naval service. He achieved instant fame with his first novel, *Lord of the Flies*, which came out in 1954 and tells the story of a group of cast-away schoolboys who quickly turn

civilised society into savagery and anarchy. Man's inherent lean-
ings towards evil are also examined under various guises in several
of his other books, including *The Spire* (1965) and *Rites of Passage*
(1980): the latter, though at one level a sea story, actually observes
mankind's progress through all the changing scenes of life, with its
comic and tragic elements interwoven, and with suffering never
far from the surface.

★   ★   ★

Poets, too, have been profoundly attracted in every age by the
tragedy of life and have experienced an overwhelming compulsion
to express it in their work. Some have done so in the specific
circumstances of suffering and death, notably such war poets as
Wilfred Owen and Edward Thomas (1914–1918) and Alun Lewis
and Keith Douglas (1939–1945). Others have produced their
work against an outwardly less traumatic background, but have
meditated on, or experienced for themselves, the pains and sorrows
of life and seen beyond them, at the point *when words fail*, the
passion and death of Jesus Christ as the ultimate 'type' of sacrifice.

The best of all forms of art seem to come out of an experience
of suffering, as if those who live 'on the edge' share a creativity
which the comfortable and conventional often lack. That this is a
reflection, a resonance, of the creativity of God in the passion of
Christ is an argument which the Christian would not find difficult
to justify.

Here, in conclusion, are two examples of such poetry which,
inadequately, will have to represent all the others. The first is separated from the second by a gap of three centuries and is one of a
group of Holy Sonnets by **John Donne**, Dean of St Paul's for the
last ten years of his life until his death in 1631:

> Death, be not proud, though some have called thee
> Mighty and dreadful, for thou art not so;
> For those whom thou think'st thou dost overthrow
> Die not, poor Death, nor yet canst thou kill me.
> From rest and sleep, which but thy pictures be,
> Much pleasure-then, from thee much more must flow;
> And soonest our best men with thee do go,
> Rest of their bones and soul's delivery.
> Thou'rt slave to fate, chance, kings and desperate men,

And dost with poison, war, and sickness dwell;
And poppy or charms can make us sleep as well,
And better than thy stroke. Why swell'st thou then?
One short sleep past, we wake eternally,
And death shall be no more. Death, thou shalt die.[6]

The second, 'Attack', is by **Siegfried Sassoon** and recalls the
sheer horror and fear experienced by a generation of young men
ordered to go out of their trenches, over the top, and into battle:

At dawn the ridge emerges massed and dun
In the wild purple of the glow'ring sun,
Smouldering through spouts of drifting smoke that shroud
The menacing scarred slope; and, one by one,
Tanks creep and topple forward to the wire.
The barrage roars and lifts. Then, clumsily bowed
With bombs and guns and shovels and battle-gear,
Men jostle and climb to meet the bristling fire.
Lines of grey, muttering faces, masked with fear,
They leave their trenches, going over the top,
While time ticks blank and busy on their wrists,
And hope, with furtive eyes and grappling fists,
Flounders in mud. O Jesus, make it stop![7]

When we find ourselves confronted personally by the mystery
of evil and undeserved suffering, we may find it helpful to turn to
the book of Job, where we read how this good and righteous man
is tested almost to the point of death:

Satan went forth from the presence of the Lord, and afflicted Job
with loathsome sores from the sole of his foot to the crown of his
head. And he took a potsherd with which to scrape himself, and sat
among the ashes.

Then his wife said to him, 'Do you still hold fast your integrity?
Curse God, and die.' But he said to her, 'You speak as one of the
foolish women would speak. Shall we receive good at the hand of
the Lord, and shall we not receive evil?' In all this Job did not sin
with his lips. (Job 2.7–10)

12 *Place*

Geography is sometimes described as the philosophy of place and there can be few people who are totally unconcerned about what one eminent geographer has called the 'whereness of things'.[1] Some would go as far as to say that an understanding of place is of fundamental importance to our entire approach to life because we are creatures of both time and space, strongly conditioned by both of them, unable to escape from them during our lifetime, and incapable of contemplating an existence in which they no longer have a part. This is why we get into such a muddle when we try to picture eternity, the state of being in which both time and space are transcended.

For the Christian, there is a fundamentally important intersection of time, space and eternity in the Incarnation, where the eternal Logos, the Second Person of the Trinity, was made man at a particular historical moment and at a specific geographical location.

Whilst geographical studies wash over onto many other academic disciplines, including astronomy, geology, sociology, politics, economics, physics and mathematics, their particular overlap with history has a very special significance for religion inasmuch as:

> certain geographic considerations combined to place the history of the little land of Palestine in the very heart of the ancient Near East. Located on the bridge between three continents, it became involved in almost every event of importance in the history of the ancient Fertile Crescent. It is not too much to say that the geographical position of this little land has always dominated its history.[2]

The implications of this in terms of biblical studies can never be far from the thoughts of anyone who seeks to know how the Christian faith developed from its Jewish roots. Nor can we proceed to consider the aesthetic consequences of place if we ignore the fact that the world is our home and that we and our total environment are inextricably interwoven, as we shall see when we think of the interaction of place with architecture, liturgy, literature, poetry, art and music.

First we need to examine the biblical concept of the 'holiness' of place. We talk in a technical sense of 'the holy places', by which we understand primarily those sites in Palestine (itself the 'Holy Land') which, because of their specific links with various incidents recorded in scripture, have become recognised as locations of particular significance for the three great monotheistic religions, Judaism, Christianity and Islam.

Jacob's reaction, on waking from his dream at Bethel, was to say:

> Surely the Lord is in this place; and I did not know it ... How awesome is this place! This is none other than the house of God, and this is the gate of heaven. (Genesis 28.16–17)

For me, this is the *locus classicus* of those places where man has become aware of a sense of the numinous, though not far behind is the experience of Moses at the 'burning bush', where God says to him:

> Do not come near; put off your shoes from your feet, for the place on which you are standing is holy ground. (Exodus 3.5)

Joshua, Moses' successor as leader of the Israelites, was greeted by a divine messenger immediately before the assault on Jericho and given a similar message:

> When Joshua was by Jericho, he lifted up his eyes and looked, and behold, a man stood before him with his drawn sword in his hand; and Joshua went to him and said to him, "Are you for us, or for our adversaries?" And he said, "No; but as commander of the army of the Lord I have now come." And Joshua fell on his face to the earth, and worshipped, and said to him, "What does my Lord bid his servant?" And the commander of the Lord's army said to Joshua, "Put off your shoes from your feet; for the place where you stand is holy". And Joshua did so. (Joshua 5.13–15)

The Psalmist also speaks of the Temple as God's 'holy place' (Psalm 24.3) and as 'the place where thy glory dwells' (Psalm 26.8). For the Jews, it was Solomon's Temple, and its successors built by Zerubbabel and Herod, which were the holy places *par excellence*. Contained within the Temple was a room of such special sanctity that it was called the most holy place.

Many other sites in Palestine were considered to be specially holy for one reason or another and those are still today regarded as centres of pilgrimage by Jews, Christians and Moslems. Other shrines which indicate that certain places are particularly valued or venerated are to be found in most parts of the world. Christians, for example, derive special inspiration from such places as Rome, Santiago de Compostela, Lourdes and Canterbury.

Places which have a significant meaning for us abound. Some may be 'holy places' in the strict sense of their being identified with some kind of religious experience; many more will be special because of their particular association with some period of our life or with some person whom we value highly; others will be special because of their natural beauty.

★   ★   ★

Architecture is clearly the aesthetic field which is most concerned with place, since what any building does is (either partially or completely) to enclose a given geographical space. The architectural historian, Ernest Short, makes this assertion:

> The basic principle of architecture is found in the capacity of matter to bear a weight and span a space. The essential forms are the column or wall which carry the weight, and the arch or beam which span the space ... The first law of architecture is that every burden must have its due support and every support its due burden.[3]

The principles, forms and laws of architecture remain unchanged, even though great changes have come about in design, materials and structural techniques. But this definition, being purely functional, makes no reference to aesthetic considerations or to the whole question of symbolism. Competent architects will have no difficulty in designing a building which will both do the job it is intended to do and stand firm for its likely life. They will also no doubt give due thought to the proper blending of mass, volume and materials, both in the building itself and in its wider context. There remains, however, that unquantifiable ingredient which marks the distinction between what is simply good and what is actually beautiful. Part of it is to do with such straightforward matters as the blending of materials and shapes and colours:

much of it is determined by the more imponderable considerations of what one guide to the appreciation of religious architecture calls:

> proportion and scale, rhythm and movement, contrasts and accentuation, axiality and symmetry.[4]

Architecture, like the other arts, is living and dynamic, and that implies change and growth. The temptation which is likely to beset any architect as he contemplates his latest commission is to fall back on what has been successful elsewhere, which may well be an entirely valid approach for someone who is designing one school after another, one hospital after another, one hypermarket after another. Even the context may not be over-important, since many such buildings now tend to be placed on greenfield sites on the edges of towns or cities. The temptation can be particularly acute for the ecclesiastical architect, as it was for his predecessors at the time of the Classical and Gothic revivals of the eighteenth and nineteenth centuries.

Serious questions must first be asked about the precise uses to which the building is to be put, questions which will elicit answers that will determine not only the details, but also the basic shape and size, of the new church or chapel. With constantly changing liturgical theories and praxis, it can no longer be assumed that the building will look much the same as a church always has done and that its fixtures and fittings will be designed and situated in similar places to those which have been familiar to generations of churchgoers. The Church is one of the most conservative institutions known to mankind, slow to take on board new ideas, slow to alter its traditions: yet the Church, if it is to be seen as a relevant part of contemporary society, rather than as an irrelevant survivor from an older era, must use the materials, resources, skills, designs and techniques of that society, where these can be positively identified as good in themselves.

There need be no conflict in principle between the architect's desire on the one hand to provide that which is physically appropriate and on the other hand to create something which will be aesthetically satisfying and which will give pleasure and stimulus to user and observer alike. If it is to be argued that beauty costs money, it must be pointed out to those who design buildings, for whatever purpose, that simplicity can itself be an expression of beauty and that there need be no fundamental polarity between what is practical and what is pleasing to the senses.

One area where this apparent dichotomy becomes more clearly focussed is where consideration has to be given to the provision of an extension to an existing building, be it an art gallery or a church, and especially where the building to be extended is designed in a very obvious style, for example Romanesque, Baroque or Georgian. The traditional tug of war between the ultra-conservatives, who will brook no alterations whatsoever, and the advocates of an undistinguished and ill-designed addition, could so easily be rendered unnecessary by a clear understanding on the part of the former as to precisely why it is necessary to extend the existing building, and a process of education for the latter on why it is essential to take into account the need for the addition to be at least in sympathy with the original, yet created both to endure and to be low in maintenance costs.

★   ★   ★

In a homily given at the Mass for Architects in Farm Street Church, London, the Abbot of Ampleforth spoke of the way in which the natural creative inspiration of man is given a richer and deeper significance for those who are open to the transcendent:

> it is enriched with a new perspective – a perspective in which the most obvious characteristic is reverence: reverence for God, reverence for man, reverence for the material used, reverence for life, reverence for the end of life, a reverence which is radically antipathetic to any shade of man-worship, of power hunger, of exploitation, of brutalism. Such reverence cannot leave things as they were, as they would have been; it comes into man's heart like the rain on the earth to make it yield a harvest of beauty and truth; and it does achieve its purpose and does make things different.[5]

This incarnational approach provides 'a sacred dimension in all creative inspiration; and all our work is conditioned by the nameless mystery that is the actual setting of our lives'. Earlier in this sermon, the Abbot had contrasted two opposing views of man's creative activity:

The first view is that man operates in a closed shop; that his achievement in creative work is the result of his own skill developed by purely human influences; that it owes nothing to any higher power which cannot be defined in purely human terms; that his work may reflect the influence of history, of technology, of social forces, of human taste, of personal idiosyncrasy: but that it does not and cannot reflect a truth, a beauty, a perspective which, in origin at least, transcends the immediate limitations of the human scene on this planet.

The second view is in sharp contrast with this. It holds that in his creative work man is vulnerable to a transcendent influence which is not of human making: that he can fight against it or ignore it or seek to control it and make it his own; but that such efforts, although they may distort his creativity, cannot in the end succeed; that man's creativity blossoms and prospers best when he is open to this transcendent influence, recognising quite simply that he is not alone in this world when inspired to make things.

It certainly adds a new perspective to those whose conditioning leads them to recognise no influences in their work beyond those which are purely human.

Cathedrals, in recent years, have become very busy places, partly in response to the increasing demands made on them for special events and by tourists and pilgrims, but also partly because they have given a great deal more thought to the identification of their proper role in today's Church and society. Even though so many of them are medieval in their foundation, various attempts have been made to overcome the restraints placed on them by their sheer size and antiquity, attempts most notably to create an appropriate 'theatre' for the production of the liturgy, which remains extremely high on the Church's agenda. The new generation of cathedrals has not readily escaped the constraints of the past, yet in buildings such as Chelmsford and Portsmouth, imaginative efforts have been rewarded by largely successful adaptations or enlargements of existing structures, to meet the needs of a Church which must for ever be looking ahead.

It is not easy to guard against the danger of becoming inward-looking by so arranging the space that the suggestion is made of a closed-in circularity. It is equally unfortunate to create the impression of a series of diminishing rectangular spaces through which one has to pass in order to reach the final target. Even though one model may properly speak of a God who is within, an immanent Lord, and the other of a God who is beyond, a transcendent Lord, the theological imperative is to express both facets of the presence of God, though not necessarily at the same time.

I have been greatly helped by both models, even in the same building. In one church, a squad of people arrived once a month on Saturday evening to reorganise the entire furniture of a large Norman nave, with a central altar being wheeled into the very middle of it and chairs placed around it on all four sides. It has to be said that not all members of the congregation enjoyed the close proximity of both the altar and their fellow-worshippers, some of whom they were actually seeing face to face during the service. Yet to many it said something very powerful about the God who is with us at the centre of our own individual worlds, a God in whose direction we all looked (symbolically, that is) from wherever we were. Then, on the following Sunday, we would find ourselves in the more familiar pattern of everyone facing east, not seeing much of one another, but focussing our gaze (again symbolically) on the God who is beyond us.

From the point of view of aesthetic 'correctness', the 'long church' mode was undoubtedly right in that place: from the point of view of those who were prepared to worship with an unconventional layout, the physical aesthetic constraints were overridden by the resulting liturgical rewards.

In an article on the understanding of liturgy in the light of its history, Professor Geoffrey Wainwright notes that worship is one of the threads which weaves in and out of the historical tapestry of the Church:

> At any given period and place, the liturgy must be seen together with doctrine, evangelism and holiness of life as composing the present and local image of the Church. The details and style of that picture will vary with time and space. Yet the present and local Church is of a piece with a Church which stretches back in time to Jesus Christ and which has been implanted in all parts of the globe.[6]

Those who have either to create or to use liturgical spaces are wise to remember that this thread of worship is strongly, but subtly, influenced by the milieu in which it occurs. The human spirit is a highly sensitive instrument capable of registering and evaluating a wide variety of impressions, each of which contributes to the ultimate experience of that worship. It has to be said that relatively few of the new church buildings erected during this century have really enabled the worshipping community to express itself liturgically in new and exciting ways. Whilst this may be less the fault of the architects than of those who commissioned them, designers must nevertheless share a fair proportion of the blame for failing to provide an appropriate contemporary theatre for the liturgy. Both the architect and the potential user require a shared vision of what they need to achieve, so that modern liturgical thinking and modern architectural practice can be brought together as the combined inspiration for the product which they both wish to produce.

The creation of an arena in which the great mystery of God can be expressed and experienced, along with a sense of the corporateness of the worshipping community, is an ideal not easily achieved, but infinitely worthwhile to pursue.

★　★　★

I do not intend to say much in this chapter about the relationship of art to buildings but it will be readily apparent that the two cannot be treated in isolation from one another, since the building has to act as the host for works of art, even if it has not been designed with that in mind, just as (ideally) the art has to be appropriate for the place in which it is located.

The actual setting of a picture or sculpture is almost as important as the work itself. Too many good sculptures, for example, are stuck in a corner of a museum, whereas they cry out to be walked around and viewed from all directions. Too many good paintings are placed so close to their neighbours, or are so badly illuminated, that much of their aesthetic appeal is negated.

Nevertheless, a large collection of paintings which either come from the same period or which illustrate a particular theme, can have a powerful effect on the onlooker and give immense aesthetic satisfaction, as may be experienced with the great collection of French Impressionist works in the Musée du Jeu de Paume in Paris. One of the problems of the modern purpose-built art gallery is that it can tend to sanitise what is exhibited there, since the works which it displays were more often than not intended for a domestic setting and would really be much more at home over the mantelpiece of the big house for which they were originally destined. However, one can be nothing but profoundly grateful to those directors and curators of our museums and art galleries, both national and local, for the painstaking care which they characteristically give to the exhibition of their treasures.

Paul Nash (1889–1946), who was to become an official artist in the Second World War, is a painter who has been described as 'uncompromisingly English'. His ability to give a sense of place to his work is seen, for example in *The Menin Road* (1918), *Sanctuary Wood, Dawn* (1917), *Chilterns Under Snow* (1923) and *Dymchurch Steps* (1923).

Many other paintings and artists are associated with particular geographical locations, such as the 'Constable' country of Suffolk, Hogarth's London, Ivon Hitchens's West Sussex and John Miller's Cornwall. So, and on a much larger scale, are very many literary works, notably poetry and novels, with their authors. Indeed, there is scarcely a county or region in the British Isles without its resident novelist or poet.

T. S. Eliot's *Four Quartets* are based on the recalling of places of significance to the writer: 'Burnt Norton', a country house famed for its roses; 'East Coker', a Somerset village once the home of the poet's ancestors; 'The Dry Salvages', a collection of rocks off the east coast of Massachusetts; and 'Little Gidding', where Nicholas Ferrar established his small Anglican community in 1625. It is in the fourth of these that appear the much-quoted lines, 'You are here to kneel where prayer has been valid'. Canon F. W. Dillistone quotes a comment made to a friend by T. S. Eliot:

> "What I mean", he said, "is that for some of us, a sense of place is compelling. If it is a religious place, a place made special by the sacrifice of a martyrdom, then it retains an aura. We know that once before a man gave of himself *here* and was accepted *here* and it was so important that the occasion continues to invest the place with its holiness. Of course, I am aware that not all persons have a sense of place, nor is it necessary for it to exist to make prayer valid!"[7]

C. P. Snow (1905–1980), in his sequence of novels *Strangers and Brothers*, explores his concern over scientific ethics whilst recalling vividly the atmosphere of the University of Cambridge from the

1920s to the 1950s. Exactly a hundred years earlier, W. Harrison Ainsworth (1805–1882) conjured up the sights and smells of bygone London in *Old Saint Paul's* and *The Tower of London*. Daphne du Maurier (1907–1989) transports us back to earlier centuries in Cornwall in *Jamaica Inn*, a tale of the early nineteenth-century and *Frenchman's Creek*, with its Restoration period background, and then brings us into the early decades of this century with *Rebecca*. Arnold Bennett (1867–1931) similarly portrays the Potteries in several of his novels, including *Anna of the Five Towns* and the *Clayhanger* trilogy.

The list is a long one, further examples being Hardy's Wessex, Scott's Border Country, H. E. Bates's Kent, Howard Spring's Manchester and Cornwall, Dickens's London, James Joyce's Dublin, James Herriott's Yorkshire Dales, Laurie Lee's Gloucestershire, Derek Tangye's West Penwith, D. H. Lawrence's Nottinghamshire, Izaak Walton's Winchester, Hilaire Belloc's Sussex, A. L. Rowse's Cornwall, Katharine Cookson's Tyne and Wear and J. B. Priestley's West Riding.

★ ★ ★

Poetry, also, has its close associations with special places. William Wordsworth (1770–1850) began to publish when he was in his early twenties, following an unhappy university career at Cambridge. After travels in Germany, he and his sister Dorothy moved to Dove Cottage, Grasmere in 1799, three years before his marriage to Mary. In 1813, the Wordsworths moved to Rydal Mount and the poet's reputation grew steadily over the following years, culminating in his appointment in 1843 as Poet Laureate. The inspiration, though not always the setting, for much of his verse was Lakeland, its scenery, its changing moods, its people, its flora and fauna.

What the Lake District was to Wordsworth and his neighbour Coleridge, so the Shropshire countryside was in even greater measure to A. E. Housman (1859–1936). His academic failure at Oxford gave no hint that he would eventually become Professor of Latin successively at University College, London and at Cambridge, though it is for his poetry that he is chiefly remembered. A wistful sadness for past joys pervades some of his work, as in these two verses:

Into my heart an air that kills
From yon far country blows:
What are those blue remembered hills,
What spires, what farms are those?

That is the land of lost content,
I see it shining plain,
The happy highways where I went
And cannot come again.

Edward Thomas (1878–1917) was one of that generation of poets whose work came to an abrupt end in the fighting of the First World War, but he is best remembered for one short work which captures the feel of a particular place on a hot summer's day:

Yes. I remember Adlestrop-
The name, because one afternoon
Of heat the express-train drew up there
Unwontedly. It was late June.

The steam hissed. Some one cleared his throat.
No one left and no one came
On the bare platform. What I saw
Was Adlestrop – only the name

And willows, willow-herb, and grass,
And meadowsweet, and haycocks dry,
No whit less still and lonely fair
Than the high cloudlets in the sky.

And for that minute a blackbird sang
Close by, and round him, mistier,
Farther, and farther, all the birds
Of Oxfordshire and Gloucestershire.

Robert Burns (1759–1796) draws his inspiration from his native Scotland and brings to it the full-blooded emotion of one with the justified reputation of a womaniser and one who knew from first-hand experience what it meant to work hard for a precarious living on the land. Fame came first with the Kilmarnock poems, written before he was 30, and a steady output of poems and songs followed to within a few months of his death from endocarditis when he was only 37. His use of Scottish dialect is a strong characteristic of his work, seen to good effect in these lines from a poem written to the memory of a mouse whose nest he disturbed with the plough:

> Week, sleekit, cow'rin', tim'rous beastie,
> O what a panic's in thy breastie!
> Thou need na start awe sae hasty,
> Wi' bickering brattle!
> I wad be laith to rin an' chase thee
> Wi' murd'ring prattle!
>
> I'm truly sorry man's dominion
> Has broken nature's social union,
> An' justifies that ill opinion
> Which makes thee startle
> At me, thy poor earth-born companion,
> An' fellow-mortal!

Sir Walter Scott (1771–1832), though best-known for his novels, also reveals his love for his native Border country in songs and poems, as this closing verse of 'Lochinvar' reveals:

> There was mounting 'mong Graemes of the Netherby clan;
> Forsters, Fenwicks, and Musgraves, they rode and they ran:
> There was racing and chasing on Cannobie Lee,
> But the lost bride of Netherby n'er did they see.
> So daring in love, and so dauntless in war,
> Have ye e'er heard of gallant like young Lochinvar?

★   ★   ★

The last area of aesthetic experience to explore under the heading of 'place' is the close relationship which music not uncommonly enjoys with specific geographical locations. The most obvious manifestation of this is to be seen in the folk music of various races and nations. In the words of the *Oxford Companion to Music*:

> There is a sense in which it may be paradoxically said that the most original composer is normally the most national, just as "the greatest genius is the most indebted man" -for, instinctively keeping himself free from conventions, he allows free play to the feelings within him, and these are necessarily largely racial and national.[8]

Although words are invaluable tools for describing places and their special meanings and associations, the composer can often add to the spoken word by means of his impressionistic skills, or even take over from the oral utterance at the point *when words fail*. Here are some examples of how a number of composers have sought to illustrate in their music some aspect of a place or country, which has made a special impact on them. The following list is, of course, highly selective and by no means comprehensive.

Bohemia, the western part of what was until recent years Czechoslovakia, has been extremely well served by a succession of composers, culminating in Bedřich Smetana (1824–1884) and Antonín Dvořák (1841–1904), and including such later ones as Janáček and Mahler though Mahler's musical inspiration is largely Austrian. Smetana was a great patriot as well as a fine musician, and was instrumental in asserting Bohemian nationality, notably through his cycle of six symphonic poems entitled *Ma vlast*, 'My Fatherland', which tell of its legends, its history and its country-side. Dvořák's *Moravian Duets* and *Slavonic Dances* brought him international acclaim and his *Gipsy Songs* add further testimony to his ability to portray his country's characteristics.

England has had far more than its fair share of composers who have sought to capture in their music the essence of their native land, or of some city or region within it. One particularly strong influence dates from the early decades of the twentieth-century, when a revival of interest in folksong coincided with the rekindling of the almost defunct flame of the glorious era of church and secular music of the sixteenth-century. Noteworthy among composers who have painted the English countryside and cityscape into their works is Arnold Bax (1883–1953), who became Master of the King's Musick, was incidentally fascinated by the folk music of Ireland, and wrote the symphonic poem, *Tintagel*. Benjamin Britten (1913–1976), among other great achievements, put East Anglia firmly on to the musical map with such works as his opera, *Peter Grimes*. George Butterworth (1885–1916), before he was killed on the Somme in the middle of the First World War, showed marked promise with *The Banks of Green Willow* and his music for the song cycle, *A Shropshire Lad*. Eric Coates (1886–1957) was responsible for a massive output of popular light music, including an evocation of the sights and sounds of the capital city in the *London Suite*.

Much of the music of Edward Elgar (1857–1934) seems to breathe the atmosphere of the English middle-west, as witness the Romano-British tale, *Caractacus,* and the oft-quoted *Enigma Variations,* though these are more a musical study of the composer's friends than of specific places. Hubert Parry (1848–1918) was another of that important group of composers whose lives spanned the Victorian and Edwardian eras. Some critics consider that he would have done a superior job with fewer, but better crafted, compositions: certainly he enjoyed setting great English words to music, as in his setting of Blake's *Jerusalem,* Milton's *Blest Pair of Sirens* or Coverdale's Psalm 122, *I was glad,* all of which possess an 'Englishness' which is as hard to define as it is distinct.

Of like eminence with Elgar stands Ralph Vaughan Williams (1872–1958), who broke much new ground whilst at the same time drawing inspiration from English folk songs and dances, and from the music of Tudor England. His topographical allusions include his *London Symphony, In the Fen Country,* three *Norfolk Rhapsodies,* the song cycle *On Wenlock Edge,* and the *Pastoral Symphony,* which breathes the very air of the English countryside: 'the Malvern Hills when viewed from afar', as Herbert Howells puts it.

There are many others, not all of them English, who have taken some aspect of the country's life or history and turned it into a musical offering. Bells, for instance, have inspired Samuel Sebastian Wesley's *Holsworthy Church Bells* or Louis Vierne's *Carillon de Westminster.*

French composers whose works reflect their national life and history include Canteloupe (1879–1957) for his *Chants d'Auvergne;* Claude Debussy (1862–1918), the musical equivalent of the Impressionist painter Monet; Marcel Dupré (1886–1971) who also turned to bells for his *Les Cloches de Perros-Guirec;* and Maurice Ravel (1875–1937) who, like Debussy, was profoundly influenced by the major French poets.

In much the same way as Bohemia was served by Smetana and Dvořák, so Bartók and Liszt expressed in their music a flavour of the national characteristics of Hungary. Béla Bartók (1881–1945) was influenced by Brahms, Liszt, Wagner and Strauss and, in partnership with Kodály, he collected some 5,000 ancient Magyar and gipsy tunes, many of which were incorporated into his major compositions. Franz Liszt (1811–1886) was a brilliant pianist as well as an innovative composer and can properly be credited with the invention of the musical genre known as the symphonic poem: his *Hungarian Rhapsodies* portray vividly the exuberant spirit of the folk music of his home country.

Scandinavian composers are not reckoned to have made many major contributions to the sum total of musical works but, as with so many of their counterparts in the other regions of Europe, the growth of nationalism in the nineteenth-century led to a resurgence of interest in the folk tunes of Denmark, Finland, Iceland, Norway and Sweden. Outstanding among the Norwegian nationalists is Edvard Greig (1843–1907) with such works as his *Norwegian Peasant March*, *Norwegian Bridal Procession*, the *Holberg Suite* and the incidental music for Ibsen's play, *Peer Gynt*. Christen Jul sums him up thus in 'Lives of the Great Composers':

> Anyone with a sense of tune will realise the charm of Greig's music and anyone who knows Norway will recognise its special character. Greig is Norway. His music is synonymous with Norwegian temper and nature, lore, light and landscape.[9]

Jean Sibelius (1865–1957) has likewise become Finland's national musical voice, reflecting in his writing the beauty of the country, together with the rigours of its long winters, as in the *Karelia Suite*, *Finlandia* and *Tapiola*, in all of which are intermingled the great legends of the land, especially the 'Kalevala'.

Scotland, also, has been depicted in music by numerous composers, through the use of folk songs, folk dances and pieces intended to paint a picture of a particular area. Lesser works include John McEwen's *Solway* Symphony and *Grey Galloway* Overture, and Hamish MacCunn's *Land of the Mountain and the Flood*, which so clearly portrays the landscape of the Scottish Highlands. Far better known are Mendelssohn's *Scottish* Symphony and his Opus 26, the Overture *The Hebrides* or 'Fingal's Cave', composed after a visit there in 1829: its second subject has been aptly described by Donald Tovey as Mendelssohn's greatest melody.

Of the many Spanish composers who have sought to express in their musical works a taste of their native land, the leading ones are Isaac Albeniz (1860–1909), with his twelve-piece suite for piano,

Iberia; Manuel de Falla (1876–1946) and his *El Retablo de Maese Pedro* and *Nights in the Gardens of Spain*; Enrique Granados (1867–1916), with his *Danses Espagnoles* and the *Goyescas*; and Felipe Pedrell (1841–1922), the founder of the modern school of Spanish nationalism and publisher of important collections of national music. Spain, perhaps more than any other country, has also been the inspirer of composers from many other lands: the long list would include Glinka's *Night in Madrid*, Lalo's *Symphonie Espagnole*, Balakirev's *Overture on Spanish Themes*, Chabrier's orchestral rhapsody *España*, Rimsky-Korsakov's *Spanish Capriccio*, Debussy's *Iberia* and Ravel's *Rapsodie espagnole*.

We turn finally to the United States of America and to a representative quartet of nineteenth and twentieth century composers who have communicated some national traits in their works, difficult as this is in a country which is so large and so varied in its racial and geographical constituents. Well embedded in the American musical tradition are the songs of Stephen Foster (1826–1864), whose work paints a musical picture of negro life in the South. Charles Ives (1874–1954), remarkable for the freedom he allows to the performer to improvise more or less at will, wrote music with such topographical titles as *Three Places in New England* and *Concord, Massachusetts*. Jazz was the chief inspiration for George Gershwin (1898–1937), much of whose music breathes the atmosphere of the 1920s and 1930s, whilst *Billy the Kid* and *Appalachian Spring* by Aaron Copland (1900–1990) incorporate elements of American folk song and cowboy music.

The list of musical compositions with geographical connections is an extensive one: the examples quoted demonstrate how in this particular aesthetic field the concept of place has been richly explored, especially in the past century and a half. Although little of it has any specifically religious overtones, much of it has the capacity to move the heart, mind and soul of the listener who is attuned to the particular topographical wavelengths: and that itself can be a religious experience, an experience in which some kind of revelation of God is made.

13 *Perfection*

'Heaven', says George Bernard Shaw, 'as conventionally conceived, is a place so inane, so dull, so useless, so miserable, that nobody has ever ventured to describe a whole day in heaven, though plenty of people have described a day at the seaside'.

The trouble with perfection is that it is indescribable, so seldom do we come across it. Shaw's somewhat ascerbic comment is too near the mark to make us feel anything other than uncomfortable. The reason for this lies not in 'heaven' itself but in what the great critic and playwright calls its conventional conception. 'Misconception' would be a far more accurate way of describing the heaven characterised by popular imagination: its inanity caused by the endless plucking of myriad harps; its dullness a result of the sheer monotony of the same boring routine; its uselessness due to the absence of anything to do but rest eternally; its misery a direct consequence of the removal of all challenge from the lives of its inhabitants.

Yet this is emphatically not the heaven of Scripture, where activity is one of its keynotes, and the worship of God the most significant component of that activity. Somewhere along the line, the Christian understanding of heaven has been derailed or shunted into a particularly curious siding. That state of perfection, which we often describe as 'heavenly', is in fact a mode of existence of which we already experience tantalising glimpses. Some of these liftings of the curtain are revealed in the beauty of nature and in those awe-inspiring natural phenomena which, though we can now explain them scientifically, still have the power to strike awe into our hearts. The sight of a volcano in full eruption or the sound of a violent thunderstorm immediately overhead, can leave few of us totally unmoved, whatever our understanding of their genesis. That, certainly, was the effect on one person of his contemplation of the sky: 'the heavens declare the glory of God and the firmament sheweth his handywork', as Coverdale translates the first verse of Psalm 19.

Immanuel Kant, the celebrated 18th-century German philosopher, looked in the same direction, but into his own soul as well, when he declared in his *Critique of Pure Reason* that:

"two things fill my mind with ever-increasing wonder and awe, the more often and the more intensely the reflection dwells on them: the starry heavens above me and the moral law within me".

As human beings, we have the innate capacity to reach for God and in doing this we are striving towards perfection. We set out on that search in many different vehicles and travel the pilgrim way using many different paths. Just occasionally, we obtain glimpses of the goal during the journey, in those moments when we seem to be taken outside ourselves, in worship, in the contemplation of some work of art, in listening to a piece of music, in pondering the words of a poem.

St Paul describes such a moment, of which he was himself presumably the subject, when that sensation of heightened awareness translated him into another mode of being:

> I know a man in Christ who fourteen years ago was caught up to the third heaven – whether in the body or out of the body I do not know, God knows. And I know that this man was caught up into Paradise – whether in the body or out of the body I do not know, God knows – and he heard things that cannot be told, which man may not utter. (2 Corinthians 12.2–4)

The Apostle is defending himself against the charge laid by his opponents of being 'unspiritual': he does not want to boast, he says, but he cannot allow the indictment to go unanswered, so he reveals this visionary experience which took place a decade and a half previously. He himself is unsure whether the experience was physical as well as psycho-spiritual, though the language he uses accords with contemporary patterns of thought which accepted the existence of a number of 'heavens', some said three, others seven. This awareness of being transported into Paradise was emphasised for him by the sound of those things 'which man may not utter'.

This was some sort of mystical experience in which, even if the soul did not achieve its ultimate aim of union with God, there was at least a vision of God, a moment of surpassing wonder and ecstasy. No one knows, because there is no objective way of measuring it either qualitatively or quantitatively, how often this kind of thing happens to human beings, quite apart that is from the false experiences achieved under the influence of drugs.

Wordsworth suggests that increasing years bring with them a diminishing return in our capacity to know such glimpses of wonder. Our own reflection will probably confirm this thought, as we dimly remember our childhood ability to dream dreams, and as we see how little we exhibit today that delightful characteristic which we call childlikeness. The opening stanza of his ode, *Intimations of Immortality from Recollections of Early Childhood*, sets the scene:

> There was a time when meadow, grove, and stream,
> The earth, and every common sight,
> To me did seem
> Apparelled in celestial light,
> The glory and the freshness of a dream.
> It is not now as it hath been of yore;-
> Turn whereso'er I may,
> By night or day,
> The things which I have seen I now can see no more.

Nearly fifty lines further on come the words, 'Heaven lies about us in our infancy!' The context in which this phrase is placed paints the wider picture:

> Our birth is but a sleep and a forgetting:
> The Soul that rises with us, our life's Star,
> Hath had elsewhere its setting,
> And cometh from afar:
> Not in entire forgetfulness,
> And not in utter nakedness,
> But trailing clouds of glory do we come
> From God, who is our home:
> Heaven lies about us in our infancy!

Not everyone would identify a time of heightened awareness with a specifically religious experience. Mary Warnock, in *Religious Imagination*, writes about C. S. Lewis,

> whose descriptions of such "epiphanies" in his autobiography, *Surprised by Joy*, are among the most vivid and memorable.

Lewis himself is careful to distinguish 'the joy of the imaginative moment from anything that he would call religion'. In a subsequent passage, Warnock observes that these powers of imagination are not given only to a single class of person:

> Such imaginative powers may be possessed by anyone; and the moments of illumination may come from nature, from personal memories, or from great works of art, music or literature. What is common to them is the feeling of infinity, of depth or height without end.[1]

★   ★   ★

Music is undoubtedly for many the primary vehicle for the transmission of those 'moments of illumination'. It is not so much that the listener sets out with the avowed intention of being transported: rather, the moment steals upon us unawares, unexpectedly. Joseph Addison, classical scholar, traveller, politician and poet of the late seventeenth and early eighteenth centuries, is perhaps guilty of overstating his case when he declares, in his *Song for St Cecilia's Day*, that music is 'the greatest good that mortals know, and all of heaven we have below', but we understand well enough what he is saying.

What goes on in the mind of the person who listens to music has its counterpart in the creative process by which that music comes to be composed. The majority of composers speak of some kind of inspiration, whether receiving from outside themselves a theme or tune, or experiencing a mood which they feel driven to express: but the fleeting thought can only be turned into music by a combination of technical skill and hard work.

The language we use to describe these processes – 'heightened awareness', 'inspiration', 'creativity', 'illumination' – can also be applied to the performance of musical works and their effect on the listener. There is all the world of difference between a very pedestrian performance of a piano concerto or operatic aria and one in which even the least modest of performers would recognise that he or she has been in some degree 'taken over'.

The listener, too, may find it hard to verbalize the process by which a performance lifts the hearer onto a plane of awareness which is not normally visited in other circumstances: yet he will know the reality of it, without necessarily understanding the psychological, emotional or spiritual forces which are at work in

153

the total experience. It may not even qualify in the technical sense as 'perfect', yet it was enough to give a foretaste of that total perfection which we are unlikely to experience on this side of death. Something happens which alters the normal way in which we perceive the stimuli of the outside world: as William Blake hints, the barriers between time and eternity, earth and heaven, are lowered:

> To see a World in a grain of sand,
> And a Heaven in a wild flower,
> Hold Infinity in the palm of your hand,
> And Eternity in an hour.

★　　★　　★

The images of 'sand' and 'flower' can be altered, *mutatis mutandis*, to symphony and fantasia or, indeed, to structure and form in sculpture. Donatello (1386–1466), the first of the early Renaissance sculptors and Cellini (1500–1571), a century or so later, were at one in their search for perfection in whatever they did, as one sees in their respective bronze works, the 'Gattamelata' and 'Perseus and Medusa'. Between them stands the towering form of Michelangelo Buonarroti (1475–1564) who possessed the highest degree of skill in architecture, engineering and painting, as well as in sculpture. From his marble 'Pietà' in St Peter's, Rome, to the Medican tombs in San Lorenzo, Florence, we see not merely beauty, but a sublime majesty of artistic expression.

Sculpture was a significant aesthetic aspect of many earlier civilisations, such as those of ancient Egypt, Assyria, China, Greece and Rome, so much so that the Greeks were believed by many to have achieved the summit of perfection in this medium. Even Michelangelo's work was considered by some of his contemporaries as sub-standard, and there still exists today in some quarters the false belief that modern sculpture, to be good, must be based on the ancient ideals. This means that a sculptor with an original turn of mind has usually found it more difficult to make a living than one who is content to reproduce copies of past glories.

What every sculptor has to decide, consciously or otherwise, is whether he or she wishes to transform the shape of some living creature, more often than not human, into a representation which cannot be other than lifeless, or to give to an inanimate substance, such as bronze or marble, those qualities which most evidently symbolize what is alive. An interesting European trio spanning the second half of the eighteenth-century and the first quarter of the nineteenth, were the Englishman John Flaxman, Jean Houdon from France and Antonio Canova of Italy, though their names may be less familiar than that of Auguste Rodin (1840–1917), the leading sculptor of his age and upon whom criticism unbounded was heaped for his frequent flouting of contemporary conventions.

Controversy has also surrounded the work of the major sculptor of the twentieth-century, Jacob Epstein (1880–1959), though a grudging acceptance of his creative genius has slowly been forth-coming over the years. Where the search for beauty has gone hand in hand with the spirit of enquiry, there we are most likely to see the most exciting results. Even though perfection is probably unattainable, the striving for it has opened the eyes of successive generations to the glories of form that stand before our very eyes. The secret of good sculpture seems to be that it can never be the product of a blueprint which creates a repeatable pattern: on the contrary, it will be unique and will be the result of careful and profound thinking.

'Sculpture', writes Sir Leigh Ashton, one-time Director of the Victoria and Albert Museum, 'sums up the main features of an epoch, and if we remain blind to its appeal, we debar ourselves from much that is most valuable in the creative achievements of the past'. These words are quoted by Dom Hubert van Zeller, who makes his own assessment thus:

> Sculpture is that arrangement of interrelating planes, masses, surfaces and lines which results in a unity corresponding to a unity which exists in the sculptor's mind. It is a certain thickness shaped at the hand of man and inspired by man's creative thought. "Thickness" demanding more than surface, "hand" demanding more than machine, "thought" demanding more than visual imagination.[2]

The author points out that it is this quality of thickness, or 'roundness', that actually makes the sculpture: the artist who is unable to judge this has only a pattern in his mind and not a design. So the elusive search for perfection in this difficult medium will once again owe whatever success it achieves at least partly to that unquantifiable element which we variously call inspiration, creativity or possession.

*　　*　　*

When we turn to consider the pursuit of perfection in art we might begin with the reminder that, whatever was once the accepted view, art seems no longer to be related to the representation of beauty. It is beyond dispute that art, and here we are thinking in particular about painting, has been a source of pleasure and enrichment since the dawn of civilisation. Through it, our eyes and our emotions are opened to enable us to perceive 'whatsoever things are lovely' (Philippians 4.8, KJV). The whole of life, with all its emotions, can be experienced through art and a very powerful communication can be established and maintained by means of it.

One of the dilemmas which confronts an artist as he or she sets out to produce something which is as near to perfection as possible, is the need to strike the right balance between tradition and creativity, between the conventional and the inspired. Should we be content with works of art which, though second-rate, are at least fresh? Here is Carl Nielsen in *My Childhood*:

> The right of life is stronger than the most sublime art, and even if we reached agreement on the fact that now the best and most beautiful has been achieved, mankind, thirsting more for life and adventure than perfection, would rise and shout in one voice: Give us something else, give us something new, indeed for Heaven's sake give us rather the bad, and let us feel that we are still alive, instead of constantly going around in deedless admiration for *the conventional*.[3]

Most of us take time to come to an appreciation of the value of art in our lives: after all, when we are young, we inhabit a world of our own, a world of heavenly unreality, in which art has little or no place. John Masefield, in *So Long to Learn*, recalls that 'in those days, as a little child, I was living in Paradise, and had no need of the arts, that at best are only a shadow of Paradise'.

It is instructive to study works of art which have an avowedly religious theme and to see how each generation has sought to encapsulate its own understanding of the perfection of beauty.

Whereas the early Christian artists of the catacombs preferred not to show God in human form, choosing instead to use such symbols as the cross or the slain lamb, the Byzantine mosaics have some superb 'portraits' of Christ. Then, from Giotto's frescos, through Leonardo da Vinci's *Last Supper* and Michelangelo's *Last Judgement*, the austere paintings of Durer and the mystical works of El Greco, the Pre-Rephaelite imaginations of Holman Hunt and Rossetti, to the drama of Stanley Spencer and the curiosities of Salvador Dali, there runs a thread of commitment, which seeks to give to each generation an understanding of what religious faith has meant to the artists.

The artist himself will sometimes speak, possibly in mystical terms, of being no longer involved in the painting once it has started to 'work' for him. He is taken over; he enters a silence which is supernatural and in which even the timescale changes. Such language is remarkably akin to that which the contemplative monk or nun will use to describe what is happening when the deeper levels of prayer are entered. Sometimes, though, the endeavour to say something different and original, using perhaps highly personalised techniques, ends up as nothing more than a form of egocentricity, rather than a genuine statement of a profound theological conviction. The present age has seen plenty of this, not only in its painting, but in its literature, music and architecture. The twentieth-century has also provided much work of real beauty and excellence in all those different fields of aesthetic concern.

*   *   *

It is sometimes said that those who are unfamiliar with the best of the world's literature, or at least that of their own country or culture, have the curtains closed across the windows of their minds and souls. Francis Bacon would have us understand the real reasons for developing an acquaintance with good literature:

> Read not to contradict nor confute, nor to believe and take for granted, nor to find talk and discourse, but to weigh and consider.

The sharpening of one's critical faculties enables one to assess what is being read, to compare it with other literary works and to make some sort of aesthetic judgement. A lifetime's reading may afford immense satisfaction, mental and spiritual, even though the reader never comes across the perfect piece of literature, whether poem, novel, drama or prose. Writers, be they poets, novelists, dramatists or essayists, may perhaps have striven for perfection, refining their work again and again, yet failing – because of their very humanity – to achieve the ultimate flawless ideal. Does such an ideal indeed exist in this world, and who is to be the final arbiter of 'correctness'?

T. S. Eliot's personal spirituality, allied to his intellectual skill and literary ability, set him apart as one who had the faculty to plumb those depths in which perfection waits to be revealed. In his analysis of religious experience and Christian faith, Canon F. W. Dillistone writes of him in these words:

> He was to be the interpreter of the deepest human emotions, the most tragic human experiences, through dramatic poetry. And ultimately, after years of struggle, this led him to the profoundest experience of all – to the still point of the turning world – to the timeless moment – the experience in which the human spirit becomes aware of the presence of that which can only be called divine.[4]

Even more significant are some words of Eliot himself in an article on religion and literature, where he speaks of the way in which what we read in works of fiction affects our own behaviour and our relationships with other people. If an author obviously approves of the conduct of the characters he has created, it can influence us to follow their example, for better or for worse. As Eliot points out:

> the author of a work of imagination is trying to affect us wholly, as human beings, whether he knows it or not; and we are affected by it, as human beings, whether we intend to be or not.

How, then, are we to undertake the pursuit of perfection when so many influences are working on us through what we read? The author answers by insisting that what we read must be examined in the light not merely of normal critical standards but, further than that, under the lamp of the principles of our faith:

What I believe to be incumbent upon all Christians is the duty of maintaining consciously certain standards and criteria of criticism over and above those applied by the rest of the world; and that by these criteria and standards everything that we read must be tested.[5]

Archbishop Robert Runcie preached a sermon on January 17th, 1985 at St Stephen's, Gloucester Road, London, to mark the twentieth anniversary of the death of T. S. Eliot. In it he said this:

Eliot has taught us the value of silence and contemplation, not as a substitute for action but as a precondition for constructive action ... He has taught us that nothing of value can be done without sacrifice, without renunciation, without the long struggle of discipleship, without the prayer for God, the infinitely suffering God, to be God in his world. Only in such a way can we arrive at "a condition of complete simplicity costing not less than everything!"[6]

There, in the still centre, we may find God; and if we find God, we find perfection. The written word of playwright, poet or novelist, without being intrinsically perfect, can be the vehicle which transports us to that costly 'condition of complete simplicity' wherein lies the perfection which constantly beckons us onwards, however frequently we may choose to ignore the outstretched hand.

Paradoxically, it is in children's literature that we can sometimes most clearly perceive this truth. Too much adult sophistication may blind us to the memory of that other condition of simplicity which we experienced in our earliest years. Books which were written specifically to enliven the religious imagination of the child or young person appeal to the part of us which still has not learnt to make hard and fast distinctions between truth and fantasy, heaven and hell, imagination and reality. One does not have to be a child to gain some spiritual insight from these books, as many will witness who did not come until adulthood to J. R. R. Tolkien's world of *The Hobbit* and *The Fellowship of the Ring*, or to C. S. Lewis's *Narnia*. Indeed, in the letter which Lewis wrote to his god-daughter, Lucy Barfield, at the start of *The Lion, The Witch and The Wardrobe*, he apologises that she is 'already too old for fairy tales ... But some day you will be old enough to start reading fairy tales again'.

$\star$ $\star$ $\star$

Saint Paul, in the most famous chapter of all his Epistles, claimed to have put childish things behind him:

> When I was a child, I spoke like a child, I thought like a child, I reasoned like a child; when I became a man, I gave up childish ways. For now we see in a mirror dimly, but then face to face. Now I know in part; then I shall understand fully, even as I have been fully understood. (1 Corinthians 13.11–12)

In this well-known passage, he writes about the greatest of the Christian virtues, faith, hope and love, and looks forward to a time when imperfections will be no more: 'When the perfect comes, the imperfect will pass away' (v. 10). The author of the last book of the Bible, the Apocalypse, also looks forward to a time when everything is gathered up into God and all is remade, though this time without imperfections:

> Then I saw a new heaven and a new earth; for the first heaven and the first earth had passed away, and the sea was no more. And I saw the holy city, new Jerusalem, coming down out of heaven from God, prepared as a bride adorned for her husband; and I heard a loud voice from the throne saying, "Behold, the dwelling of God is with men. He will dwell with them, and they shall be his people, and God himself will be with them; he will wipe away every tear from their eyes, and death shall be no more, neither shall there be mourning nor crying nor pain any more, for the former things have passed away." (Revelation 21.1–5)

Although Christians share this vision of a future when all will be good and true and beautiful, where faith, hope and love are the reigning virtues, they have not usually taken it to be an adequate excuse for doing nothing to further the work of the Kingdom of God in this world and in this life. Jesus himself has some terse and compelling words to say on this matter: 'You must be perfect, as your heavenly Father is perfect' (St Matthew 5.48) and he instructs us to pray to that Father in heaven, saying, 'hallowed be thy name, thy kingdom come, thy will be done, on earth as it is in heaven'. The meaning of that final phrase is made clearer when it is attached to each of the three preceding petitions and not just to the last one, *viz*:

hallowed be thy name, on earth as it is in heaven;
thy kingdom come, on earth as it is in heaven;
thy will be done, on earth as it is in heaven.

Mystics, as well as Christian activists, have usually realised the need for faith to be earthed in the realities of the world. Henry Wadsworth Longfellow (1807–1882), the great linguistic scholar from New England, famed for such works as *Hiawatha* and *The Courtship of Miles Standish*, and less well known for his religious dramatic cycle *Christus*, wrote in *Michael Angelo*, 'You would attain to the divine perfection and yet not turn your back upon the world'.

Francis Thompson (1859–1907) is best remembered for his poem, *The Hound of Heaven*, in which he paints a picture, in language somewhat reminiscent of the seventeenth-century English mystical poets, of the human soul being chased, or hounded, by God. In another of his works, *The Kingdom of God*, he has a much more down to earth and memorable couplet in which he writes of 'the traffic of Jacob's ladder, pitched between Heaven and Charing Cross'. A remarkably similar piece of imagery is used by G. K. Chesterton in *The Rolling English Road*: 'For there is good news yet to hear and fine things to be seen, before we go to Paradise by way of Kensal Green'.

More than one writer, however, has reminded us that we are all capable of creating our own heaven or hell, without waiting for the final judgement and the ultimate separation of wheat and tares. Thus Nikos Kazantzakis in *The Last Temptation*: 'The doors of heaven and hell are adjacent and identical: both green, both beautiful'. A much profounder thought underlies John Milton's words: 'The mind is its own place, and in itself can make a heav'n of hell, a hell of heav'n' (*Paradise Lost*, I, 253).

This book is concerned with knowing God through things of beauty, therefore we shall need to take cognizance of the beauty of a life which is lived as closely as possible to God, responding to his call to perfection. St Paul and St John, have much to say in their different ways about the three great Christian virtues, faith, hope and love, which make the living of that life possible and enable us to move more closely to God.

St Paul brings them all together in one sentence:

So faith, hope, love abide, these three; but the greatest of these is love. (1 Corinthians 13.13)

St John, also, has much to say about each of them. In the original ending of the Gospel which bears his name, he explains the reason for his having written it:

Now Jesus did many other signs in the presence of the disciples, which are not written in this book; but these are written that you may believe that Jesus is the Christ, the Son of God, and that believing you may have life in his name. (St John 20.30–31)

Although John does not use the word 'hope' in his Gospel (though see 1 John 3.3), it is nevertheless implicit in much of what he writes, for example his promise that 'in my Father's house are many rooms; if it were not so, would I have told you, that I go to prepare a place for you?' (St John 14.2). The Gospel, the Epistles and the Revelation all contain numerous references to love: in these two verses, the word 'love' is used as both noun and verb:

Beloved, let us love one another; for love is of God, and he who loves is born of God and knows God. He who does not love does not know God; for God is love. (1 John 4.7–8)

As for the three ancient ideals of goodness, truth and beauty, what both Paul and John do is to give them a new significance by metamorphosing them into three other words, which give them a new sense of vigour. Alfred W. Pollard explains this in some thoughts on 'The Artist and the Saint':

Transmute beauty into Life (zoe), transmute truth into Light (phos), transmute goodness (or righteousness) into Love (agape), and the words become energizing and creative.[7]

The same writer adds shortly afterwards:

All the reality of Religion and Art and Science comes from the interaction of the ideals expressed in these six words. The three we take as our tests, Beauty, Truth and Goodness, must be always challenging each other to make sure that the Beauty is really beautiful, the Truth is really true and the Goodness is really good.

Writing a century ago in his outline of aesthetic theory, George Santayana grapples with the problems of the beauty of form, acknowledges that 'beauty as we feel it is something indescribable' and boldly declares that it is 'the clearest manifestation of perfection and the best evidence of its possibility'.[8]

Christians can happily associate themselves with this sentiment, having first acknowledged that God himself is the author of beauty, that the beauty is revealed in its fullest form in the life and person of Jesus Christ, and that the same beauty is manifested through the Holy Spirit in the exercise of faith, hope and love. Sometimes it is the apprehension of virtue that brings us to a sense of penitence. When we see more clearly the beauty of God, we are convinced of the ugliness of sin; when we see the truth of God, falseness stands exposed; when we see the goodness of God, we become aware of how far we fall short of it; and when we begin to look for something to remedy this, we are led to the Christian doctrine of the forgiveness of sins.

Anthony de Mello, the Indian-born Jesuit priest and teacher of spirituality, has this dialogue in one of his books of meditations, under the heading of 'Love's Forgetfulness':

> Sinner: "Remember not my sins, O Lord!"
>
> Lord: "What sins? You'll have to prod my memory, I forgot them long ago".[9]

Sometimes we are unable to hear and accept the forgiveness of God because we allow no opportunity in our lives for times of silence, for it is frequently in those moments of stillness that the voice of God can be heard most clearly. Elijah discovered this when, after all the hubbub, turmoil and commotion of his confrontation on Mount Carmel with the prophets of the false god, Baal, he withdrew into the solitude of the wilderness near Beersheba:

> And behold, the Lord passed by, and a great and strong wind rent the mountains, and broke in pieces the rocks before the Lord, but the Lord was not in the wind; and after the wind an earthquake, but the Lord was not in the earthquake; and after the earthquake a fire, but the Lord was not in the fire; and after the fire a still small voice. (1 Kings 19.11b–12)

This has been the experience of Christians, too, who have retreated, temporarily or permanently, from the hustle and bustle of the everyday world, to find silence in the presence of God, whether in the quiet of a monastery or convent, or in the snatched moments of stillness in a busy day. It is then that we may find ourselves liberated sufficiently to bring our subconscious mind into the awareness of God's being. When this happens, we are able, as Isaiah says, 'to wait upon the Lord' in quietness and confidence and so are more likely to hear the word of his forgiveness, which then frees us to hear so much more as well.

The Christian never actually arrives, at least not in this world, at the ultimate destination, the full vision of God in unclouded glory. We are always a pilgrim people, travelling hopefully, never asserting that we have achieved perfection, though ever striving towards it, and so often sustained on our journey by those experiences which light upon us *when words fail*.

14 *Postlude*

It is a great privilege to share regularly in the worship of a cathedral. Most of them enjoy the advantages of space, architectural splendour and the valuable twin resources of manpower and music. That experience has been one of the major components in shaping the way in which I comprehend the Christian faith. This is because I believe that one's faith is conditioned to a considerable degree by one's understanding of, and participation in, liturgy; conversely, our faith finds a reflection in our worship. This interweaving and interpenetration of faith and liturgy, of doctrine and worship, are also determinants in much else of what we do and are, and in our whole approach to life.

Towards the end of his fascinating study, *The Identity of Christianity*, Stephen Sykes, having quoted the Latin tag, *lex orandi, lex credendi* (literally, law of praying, law of believing), re-poses the perennial question as to whether worship should provide the criteria for doctrine or doctrine for worship. But, he maintains, it is a confused question in that there is an incomparability between the two. So he suggests that, in practice,

> the dispute between these supposed alternatives has resolved itself into a contrast and comparison, not between doctrine and worship, but between doctrine and liturgies. Here the situation is much plainer, since liturgical texts and doctrinal texts are comparable entities, and it can be reasonably asked whether, for example, a reference to a liturgical text constitutes an appropriate argument in doctrine, and vice versa.[1]

The conclusion to which he comes is that 'all Christian doctrinal belief is worshipping belief'.[2]

Worship can lead us to a fuller understanding of the meaning of the doctrinal statements that we affirm in the Christian creeds. One reason for this is to be found in the symbolism, verbal or material, with which our liturgies abound. In the first category are richly suggestive words such as body, blood, water, mystery, glory, salvation and communion. The second includes water, bread, wine, the cross, incense, colour, vestments, lights and processions.

In our worship, liturgical and private, we make our answer to

God: we reflect, no doubt imperfectly, what we comprehend theologically of him. There need be no physical element in it whatsoever, no sound, no speech, no movement: yet our humanity is such that it will normally be quickened to devotion by those words, symbols and actions which customarily accompany public worship.

Liturgy has a further function, too, in being an outward sign of the unbroken tradition of worship, which has been a characteristic of the life of the Church throughout its history. Rites and ceremonies, language and actions, come and go over the centuries. The liturgy itself continues unceasingly and when we **do** the liturgy, we associate ourselves with Christians of all other ages and cultures as well as with the God of the present moment. The one whom we worship, however, is the mystery which defies definition:

> We must always remember that the Being of God is a mystery. We are bidden to "worship" not to understand "the Unity in Trinity and Trinity in Unity". Whenever the mind comes into contact with reality it is baffled by a sense of mystery. Much more must it be so when it comes into contact with God, the ultimate reality.[3]

* * *

The question which this book has been addressing is not only how we can know God, but how the things of beauty can bring us into the right state of being, preparatory to our knowing him. At its heart, it is a question about faith as much as it is one about epistemology and aesthetics, for it is through faith that we know God. Hand in hand with faith goes a willingness to do the will of God, in so far as we are able to understand it and in so far as our human frailty will permit it. This in turn depends partly on our psychological predispositions and partly on our intellectual perceptions.

> Faith is obedience; it is not an imaginative spree, an orgy of credulity. We are not called upon to believe the incredible. ... But we only want to believe if our mind is satisfied that we ought to believe. Ultimately faith must be not an indulgence in pleasing fantasy but the surrender to an existential necessity.[4]

We are challenged to examine the evidence, as far as we are able, so that we can determine for ourselves whether or not it has the ring of truth. Our faith can be stimulated by those signs and symbols which art in all its forms pushes into our consciousness, or indeed into those deeper layers of our subconscious or unconscious. Sometimes these aesthetic triggers will do much more than give us pleasure or 'heightened awareness': they may disturb or move us sufficiently for us to feel compelled to act on them. In the concluding chapter of *Art and the Question of Meaning*, Hans Küng states that art can be a great symbol:

> a symbol which, despite all difficulties and opposition, can remind us human beings of the great heritage of the past, the future still to be won, of the meaning, value, and dignity of our life here and now; a symbol that can rouse our passion for freedom and truthfulness, our hunger for justice and love, our yearning for fellowship, reconciliation, and peace.[5]

The qualities described here are very much in accord with the guiding principles upon which Christians have founded their lives since the time of Jesus himself. Sometimes art goes beyond the gift of aesthetic satisfaction in another direction and allows the artist and/or the viewer to affirm those intrinsic truths which we normally associate with the activity of our souls. The painter, for example, seeing more deeply into the reality of the subject, can enable us to look not merely with our outward eyes but with spiritual insight as well, so that we perceive things from a different angle and acquire a new vision of what till now has been ordinary or even unnoticed. This can lead to a growing awareness of the underlying unity of art and religion and life itself.

Tainted art, of any kind, can actually prevent our perception of this unity: because it is not an expression of truth, it cannot minister adequately to our mental or spiritual health. This will not prevent a wide variety of interpretation of goodness, truth and beauty, for subjective judgements are being made all the time, even by those who think they are being wholly objective. In the last resort, we have to acknowledge our limitations whilst at the same time endeavouring to expand our aesthetic and spiritual horizons.

Thus beauty and faith become close companions on a journey which is not be thought of as concerned only with the workings of mind and body: it is the pilgrimage of a soul as well. It is, furthermore, part of our response to that question of Jesus, 'Who do men say that I am?' When with St Peter we reply, 'You are the Christ', we make an act of faith in the one who, as well as being the Way, the Truth and the Life, is equally the author and giver of all that is good, beautiful and truthful.

It goes without saying that there are millions of people in this world who either have no knowledge of Christ or who have rejected him, but who nevertheless experience a full measure of aesthetic satisfaction when they read poetry, watch plays, listen to music, examine sculpture, visit art galleries, marvel at architectural splendours or enjoy a good sunset. St Paul on his visit to Athens was well aware that he was in a university city and the world's greatest centre of the arts. Athene, its patron goddess, was herself the patroness of the arts and it was from here that the finest literature and sculpture in the world had emerged.

While the Apostle was waiting at Athens for the arrival of Silas and Timothy, he reacted strongly to the presence of all the idols in the city and preached 'Jesus and the resurrection'. The intelligentsia of the city took him to the Areopagus and asked him about this strange new teaching which he was giving. St Luke, the author of the 'Acts of the Apostles', adds this:

> All the Athenians and foreigners who lived there spent their time in nothing except telling or hearing something new. (Acts 17.21)

So there, in the middle of the Areopagus, Paul observes that he has come across an altar with the inscription, **TO AN UNKNOWN GOD**. He then proclaims that God, far from being unknown, created the world and everything in it, and raised Jesus from the dead. There, on that rocky height, named after the Greek god of war, Ares, and before the most respected of all the Athenian courts, the Gospel of Jesus Christ was preached within sight of the exquisite Acropolis and the glorious bronze Minerva:

> Paul, standing in the middle of the Areopagus, said: "Men of Athens, I perceive that in every way you are very religious. For as I passed along, and observed the objects of your worship, I found also an altar with this inscription, "To an unknown god." What therefore you worship as unknown, this I proclaim to you. (Acts 17.22–23)

His speech on this occasion was full of literary allusions and would have registered immediately in the minds of the cultured listeners. In essence, it was the Good News of the Kingdom of God, with its concomitant call for belief and repentance and closely parallel to some words in the opening chapter of St Mark's Gospel:

> Jesus came into Galilee, preaching the gospel of God, and saying, "The time is fulfilled, and the kingdom of God is at hand; repent, and believe in the gospel". (St Mark 1.14b–15)

The philosophers who heard Paul speaking had dedicated their lives to the pursuit of truth and were privileged to do it here amid some of the most beautiful things which had ever been assembled in any one place. They would consider themselves to be exemplars of a code of ethics, whether Stoic or Epicurean, which they believed led them to goodness, either through the search for virtue or through the pursuit of pleasures. Sadly, Paul seems to have made little impact on his hearers, who virtually laughed him out of court when he spoke of the resurrection of the dead. Looking back on his Athenian visit many years later, he is able to ask:

> Where is the wise man? Where is the scribe? Where is the debater of this age? Has not God made foolish the wisdom of the world? ... For Jews demand signs and Greeks seek wisdom, but we preach Christ crucified, a stumbling block to Jews and folly to Gentiles, but to those who are called, both Jews and Greeks, Christ the power of God and the wisdom of God. For the foolishness of God is wiser than men, and the weakness of God is stronger than men. (1 Corinthians 1.20–25)

This is one of the paradoxes of the Christian life and a constant reminder that man's false pride in his wisdom looks absurdly pathetic in the light of the Cross. It is faith in Jesus Christ, crucified and risen, which is the gateway to salvation. St Paul would have us believe that our knowledge of God does not come through pagan philosophical speculation and enquiry. How, then, can we know God?

We have seen in this book that as well as the obvious 'religious' ways of seeking to know God, such as prayer and worship, Word and Sacrament, or the study of theology, we can identify many other windows which have the power to open the mind and soul

169

through aesthetic appreciation: literature (drama, poetry, novels, essays), architecture and sculpture, painting and music.

Paul does not rule out 'wisdom' as a word never to be used about God. In his letter to the Colossians, written partly to counter the Gnostic heresy, he equates divine Wisdom, understood by the Jews to be the agent of creation, with the Cosmic Christ:

> He is the image of the invisible God, the first-born of all creation; for in him all things were created, in heaven and on earth, visible and invisible, whether thrones or dominions or principalities or authorities – all things were created through him and for him. He is before all things, and in him all things hold together. (Colossians 1.15–17)

One of the most significant words in that quotation is 'image', or 'eikon' in the original Greek text. It sets off reverberations in a number of directions: back to the Old Testament and the concept of the divine Wisdom, subsequently revealed perfectly in Jesus; back further to the Creation story in Genesis, where God creates man in his own image (eikon), a reminder of what man was intended to be; back to the Greek philosophers, who also used the word eikon to describe the Logos, or Word, of God. It is the same word which is used today for those paintings of Jesus or of one of the Christian saints which have until recently been specially associated with the Eastern Orthodox Church but which have now become part of the spiritual currency of western christendom as well. Whilst they are not worshipped in themselves, they give rise to intense veneration, and the very execution of such works is seen as a form of prayer, yet they remain images, icons, representations of the likeness of the incarnate Lord, of his Mother, or of one of the other saints.

Only Jesus himself, as St Paul explained in his speech at Athens, reveals God fully, the god who to those Athenians was 'unknown'. In another New Testament letter, the author describes Jesus as the one who 'reflects the glory of God and bears the very stamp of his nature' (Hebrews 1.3). The word which is translated as 'stamp' is the word 'character', which here has the connotation of a seal, in the sense that it is a true likeness or expression of the original. So, when we look at Jesus, we see the exact image of God. Works of art, be they paintings, sculptures or icons, can produce a likeness of God, a representation of what the artist wishes to portray about God, and they can be a powerful means of showing us aspects of God which we may never otherwise have considered. Always they fall short of the original and we have to go back again to Jesus for that one truly faithful reproduction. St Paul was equally aware of this: in another of his epistles he described Christ as 'the likeness of God', where again the original word is 'eikon' (2 Corinthians 4.4).

At the end of the Prologue to his Gospel, St John uses a different thought-form to express the same truth:

> No one has ever seen God; the only son, who is in the bosom of the Father, has made him known. (St John 1.18)

This is a key theme of the fourth Gospel: if you want to know what God is like, look at Jesus and you will see. To Jew and Gentile alike, God was usually believed to be remote, hidden, inaccessible, unapproachable, unattainable. Now he is so no longer: he is revealed, incarnate, in Jesus of Nazareth.

For the artist today the question remains: How **do** you depict the image of Christ? The wonderful paintings of Giotto, made at a time when very few people could read, are unrepeatable. His stunning depiction of the kiss of Judas is totally lacking in sentiment: as we would say today, it is eyeball to eyeball stuff. It is a gigantic drama being enacted before our very eyes and in its time must have been the equivalent of a three-hour television play. Now, with the unceasing impact of advertising, of television, of weekend supplements, and of images shrieking at us from all directions, the painter and the sculptor increasingly find themselves turning in alternative directions as they search for other ways of speaking the truth.

The ultimate mystery of God always remains. It must also be so in those lesser revelations provided for us by artists, musicians, sculptors and writers and by all others who help us to articulate something within us, *when words fail*. The wise will be thankful for each glimpse which they provide, because all manifestations of beauty are, at their source, revelations of God.

REFERENCES

The notes for each chapter refer to the authors in the Bibliography on pages 175 to 178.

1 Prelude
1   Happold, p.19
2   Baillie, p.v

2 Panorama
1   Platten, p.14
2   Flew, p.194
3   Whittle, p.3
4   Storr, p.188
5   Fraser, p.2

3 Pilgrimage
1   Burrell, p.1
2   Coghill, p.25
3   Eliot, p.273
4   Davies, R., p.68
5   Küng, (1977), p.70
6   Lake, p.15
7   Wilson, p.13

4 Personality
1   Richardson and Bowden (1969), p.242
2   Hanson, A. T. and R. P. C., p. 1
3   Mackey (1987), p.8
4   Lewis (1958), p.43
5   Tennyson and Ericson, p.27
6   Jones, D. (1937), p. 135
7   Allchin, p.284

5 Power
1   Rahner, p.54
2   Jones, Wainwright and Jarrold, p.532
3   Bicknell, p.28
4   Archbishops' Commission (1938), p.40
5   Küng (1981), p.39

6 Paradox
1   Balthasar, vol. iii, p.24

2   Perry, p.18
3   Jones, Wainwright and Jarrold, p.495
4   Mellers, p.159
5   Tillich, p.177
6   Routley, p.30

7   Philosophy
1   Balthasar, vol. iv, p.19
2   Lacey, p.15
3   Flew, p.39
4   Zeller, p.93
5   Küng (1981), p.22
6   Cook, p.125
7   Binney and Pearce, p.30

8   Partnership
1   Scott, W., p.xxxi

9   Prayer
1   Buchanan, Lloyd and Miller, p.40
2   Underhill, p.x
3   Jeffery, p.20
4   Archbishops' Commission (1992), p.33
5   Archbishops' Commission (1992), p.70
6   Phillips, p.236
7   Booty, p.6
8   Drury (1972), p.34

10   Proclamation
1   Bowden, p.116
2   Harries, p.78
3   Shearlock (1990), p.17
4   Day (1984), p.39
5   Abrams and Hutchinson, p.5
6   Hamlyn, p. 273
7   Maquet, p.2
8   Whittle, p.53
9   Drury (1983), p.1
10   Scholes, p.184
11   Balthasar, vol. 3., p.391
12   Gardner, W. H., pp.14 and 20
13   Gardner, W. H., p.30
14   Betjeman, p.41
15   Thomas, R. S., p.81

11 Passion

1 Shearlock (1984), p.15
2 Hick, p.279
3 Lewis (1940), p.103
4 Platten, p.18
5 Vance (1983), p.283
6 Gardner, H., p.197
7 Larkin, p.203

12 Place

1 Debenham, p.12
2 Aharoni, p.xi
3 Short, p.xiv
4 Davies, J. G., p.244
5 Barry, p.2
6 Jones, Wainwright and Jarrold, p.495
7 Dillistone, p.93
8 Scholes, p.673
9 Bacharach, vol. 3, p.92

13 Perfection

1 Mackey (1986), p.150
2 Zeller, p.23
3 Cohen, p.167
4 Dillistone, p.55
5 Tennyson and Ericson, p.28
6 Runcie, p.271
7 Dearmer, p.133
8 Santayana, p.269
9 de Mello, p.123

14 Postlude

1 Sykes, p.277
2 Sykes, p.278
3 Bicknell, p.68
4 Hanson, R. P. C., p.68
5 Küng (1981), p.54

BIBLIOGRAPHY

Abrams, R. I. and Hutchinson, W. A. (1982) *An Illustrated Life of Jesus*, Abingdon Press

Aharoni, Y. (1979) *The Land of the Bible*, Burns and Oates

Allchin, A. (*Theology*, June 1973) *A Discovery of David Jones*

Archbishops' Commission on Church Music (1992) *In Tune with Heaven*, Church House Publishing and Hodder and Stoughton

Archbishops' Commission on Christian Doctrine (1938) *Doctrine in the Church of England*, SPCK

Bacharach, A. L. ed. (1943) *Lives of the Great Composers*, Penguin Books

Baillie, J. (1939) *Our Knowledge of God*, Oxford University Press

Balthasar, H. U. von (1984) *The Glory of the Lord*, T. and T. Clark

Barry, P. (*Church Building*, Autumn 1990) *Creativity and Transcendence*

Betjeman, J. (1981 *Church Poems*), later in *Collected Poems, 1909–1962*, John Murray

Bicknell, E. J. (1946) *A Theological Introduction to the Thirty-Nine Articles of the Church of England*, Longmans

Binney, M. and Pearce, D. ed. (1979) *Railway Architecture*, Orbis Publishing Ltd.

Booty, J. (1983) *Meditating on Four Quartets*, Cowley

Bowden, A. (*Theology*, March 1986) *Homage to Chagall the Theologian*

Buchanan, C., Lloyd, T. and Miller, H. (1980) *Anglican Worship Today*, Collins

Bungay, S. (1984) *Beauty and Truth*, Oxford University Press

Burrell, A. ed. (1908) *Canterbury Tales* (Geoffrey Chaucer), J. M. Dent & Sons Ltd.

Coghill, N. trans. (1951) *The Canterbury Tales* (Geoffrey Chaucer), Penguin Books

Cohen, J. M. and M. J. (1976) *A Dictionary of Modern Quotations*, Penguin Books

Cook, R. (1974) *The Tree of Life*, Thames and Hudson

Davies, J. G. (1982) *Temples, Churches and Mosques*, Blackwell

175

Davies, R. (1983) *The Deptford Trilogy*, Penguin Books

Day, M. (1984) *Modern Art in English Churches*, Mowbray

Dearmer, P. ed. (1924) *The Necessity of Art*, SCM Press

Debenham, F. (1950) *The Use of Geography*, English Universities Press

de Mello, A. (1984) *The Song of the Bird*, Doubleday

Dillistone, F. W. (1981) *Religious Experience and Christian Faith*, SCM Press

Drury, J. (1972) *Angels and Dirt*, Darton Longman and Todd

Drury, J. (*Theology*, January 1983) *Who's Afraid of Richard Wagner*

Eliot, T. S. (1935) *Murder in the Cathedral*, Faber and Faber

Eliot, T. S. (1969) *The Complete Poems and Plays*, Faber and Faber

Flew, A. (1984) *A Dictionary of Philosophy*, Macmillan

Foster, J. R. (1963) *Modern Christian Literature*, Burns and Oates

Fraser, H. (1986) *Beauty and Belief*, Cambridge University Press

Gardner,H. ed. (1979) *The New Oxford Book of English Verse*, Oxford University Press

Gardner, W. H. ed. (1953) *Poems and Prose of Gerard Manley Hopkins*, Penguin Books

Hamlyn (1964) *Art Treasures of the World*, Hamlyn

Hanson, A. T. and R. P. C. (1980) *Reasonable Belief*, Oxford University Press

Hanson, R. P. C. (1976) *Mystery and Imagination*, SPCK

Happold, F. C. (1968) *The Journey Inwards*, Darton Longman and Todd

Harries, R. (1993) *Art and the Beauty of God*, Mowbray

Hick, J. (1968) *Evil and the God of Love*, Fontana

Jefferey, P. (*Concilium*, 2/1989) *Chant East and West*

Jones, C., Wainwright, G. and Jarrold, E. (1978) *The Study of Liturgy*, SPCK

Jones, D. (1937) *In Parenthesis*, Faber and Faber

Küng, H. (1977) *On Being a Christian*, Collins

Küng, H. (1981) *Art and the Question of Meaning*, SCM Press

Lacey, A. R. (1976) *A Dictionary of Philosophy,* Routledge and Kegan Paul

Lake, F. (1966) *Clinical Theology*, Darton Longman and Todd

Larkin, P. ed. (1973) *The Oxford Book of Twentieth Century English Verse*, Oxford University Press

Lewis, C. S. (1940) *The Problem of Pain*, HarperCollins

Lewis, C. S. (1958) *Reflections on the Psalms*, HarperCollins

Mackey, J. P. ed. (1986) *Religious Imagination*, English Universities Press

Mackey, J. P. (1987) *Modern Theology*, Oxford University Press

Maquet, J. (1986) *The Aesthetic Experience*, Yale University Press

Mellers, N. (*Church Building*, date unknown) *Bach and the Dance of God*, Faber and Faber

Perry, M. (1977) *The Paradox of Worship*, SPCK

Phillips, C. H. (1945) *The Singing Church*, Faber and Faber

Platten, S. (*The Modern Churchman*, vol. xxviii, no. 1, 1985), *Thomas Hardy's Flawed Universe*

Rahner, K. (1978) *Foundations of Christian Faith*, Darton Longman and Todd

Richardson, A. and Bowden, J. (1983) *A New Dictionary of Christian Theology*, SCM Press

Routley, E. (1980) *Church Music and the Christian Faith*, Collins

Runcie, R. A. K. (*Theology*, July 1985) *The Twentieth Anniversary of the Death of T. S. Eliot*

Santayana, G. (1896) *The Sense of Beauty*, Scribners

Scholes, P. A. (1978) *The Oxford Companion to Music*, Oxford University Press

Scott, W. *Oliver Goldsmith*: quoted from his 'Lives of the Novelists' (1821–24) in *The Vicar of Wakefield*, Thomas Nelson and Sons Ltd.

Shearlock. D. J. (1984) *Romsey Abbey*, Pitkin Pictorials Ltd.

Shearlock, D. J. (1990) *The Practice of Preaching*, Churchman Publishing

Short, E. R. (1936) *A History of Religious Architecture*, Philip Allan

Storr, A. (1992) *Music and the Mind*, Harper Collins

Sykes, S. (1984) *The Identity of Christianity*, SPCK

Tennyson, G. B. and Ericson, E. E. Jr. ed. (1975) *Religion and Modern Literature*, Eerdmans

Thomas, R. S. (1981) *Between Here and Now*, Macmillan

Tillich, P. (©1959) *The Courage to Be*, Yale University

Underhill, E. (1911) *Mysticism*, Methuen

Vance, N. (*Theology*, November 1981) *Iris Murdoch's Serious Fun*

Vance, N. (*Theology*, July 1983) *Corruption and Grace in Graham Greene*

Whittle, D. (1966) *Christianity and the Arts*, Mowbray

Wilson, J. (1958) *Language and Christian Belief*, Macmillan

Zeller, H. van (1960) *Approach to Christian Sculpture*, Sheed and Ward

SCRIPTURE REFERENCES

Unless otherwise stated, all Scripture quotations are from RSV *Common Bible* © copyright 1973 by Division of Christian Education of the National Council of the Churches of Christ in the United States of America and published in Great Britain by Harper Collins.

Index

180

INDEX